# Sometimes I Haven't Got a Prayer

## And Other "Real" Catholic Adventures

# Sometimes I Haven't Got a Prayer

## And Other "Real" Catholic Adventures

Mary Kavanagh Sherry

**Resurrection Press**
An Imprint of
CATHOLIC BOOK PUBLISHING CO.
Totowa • New Jersey

# DEDICATION

*To Maureen, Tom, John, Syphachanh,*
*Bob and Sheila*

— · — · — · — · — · —

First published in March, 2003 by

Catholic Book Publishing/Resurrection Press

77 West End Road

Totowa, NJ 07512

ISBN 1-878718-83-5 (h/c)

ISBN 1-878718-79-7 (p/b)

Library of Congress Catalog Card Number: 2002115853

Cover design by Beth DeNapoli

Cover art by Mary Southard, CSJ, © Sisters of St. Joseph of La Grange

Printed in Canada

1 2 3 4 5 6 7 8 9

# Contents

*". . . You who need nobody's service, can use anybody's. So I would ask that, among all the millions of souls you cherish, some few, upon the occasion of reading (this), may learn to understand you a little, and to love you much."*

—*Ronald A. Knox*

# Acknowledgements

I AM grateful to Maria Kavanagh, my mother, for her encouragement and counsel and for passing on the writing gene; to Mary Ann and George Schwane for their advice during the conceptual stage; to Beth Bender and Mary Sue Goss, who stimulated my thinking and corrected the proofs; to the people, mentioned in these essays, who have provoked insights over the course of many years; and to Emilie Cerar of Resurrection Press, for motivating me and skillfully editing my work.

I am further indebted to the members of my parish, Mary, Mother of the Church, in Burnsville, Minnesota, whose enthusiastic response to "True Confession" in the parish newsletter rekindled my desire to write; and to Father Jim Zappa, our pastor, who did so much to stoke the spiritual fire I needed to finish this work.

Thanks is due, as well, to the editors of the following publications, in which versions of several chapters in this book were originally published, including:

"True Confession," *America,* November 19, 2001.

"Fasting? But It's So . . . Mortifying!" *America,* March 4, 2002.

"What Power? Whose Glory?" *America,* December 2, 2002.

"Offer-It-Up? Oh, Sure . . . Right!" and "Sometimes Your Best Friends DO Tell You," to be published in *America,* 2003.

"Learning from the Good Who Didn't Die Young," which appeared as "Learning to Love the Old," *St. Anthony Messenger,* April, 1977.

"Why Me, Lord?" *Sign,* December, 1980/January, 1981.

# Foreword

THERE is no end of good, sober reasons to be Catholic and remain Catholic from the cradle to the grave. The reasons on this list are logical, theological, psychological, sociological, intellectual, and imaginative. One reason for being and remaining Catholic, however, you don't hear much about. It would make a great bumper sticker: "Catholics Have More Fun!"

Oops, does this sound scandalous? Do I make too light of a profound and serious matter? Do I trivialize the Catholic faith which is deep and complex? Perhaps not. For the main reason Catholics have more fun is that Catholics—if their faith is grown-up and healthy—don't take their religion too seriously. No matter how serious and sober-minded Catholics are about their religion there comes a point where they throw up their hands and burst out laughing the laugh of the joyful and the innocent.

For Catholics, you see, take seriously the simple fact that their religion is not and never can be an absolute in itself. For Catholics, religion—from the folksiest traditions to the most profound doctrines—is merely a means to an end. Our religion isn't our God. On the contrary, only God can be God, and the Catholic faith and way of life takes seriously the need to let God be God. The great early twentieth-century Catholic convert G.K. Chesterton scored a bull's-eye when he said that it's the sign of a healthy religion when you can joke about it.

All that said, it's also true that the genius of Catholicism is in what's called "the sacramental principle," which means that Catholics can find God everywhere and any-where, around every corner and under every leaf. It's a truism to say that God is reflected in his Creation. Only hard-core atheists and agnostics do not see God in a beautiful sunset, or the flowers that spring up in the deserts, or in a baby's gurgling smile. But Catholics find God not only in nature but Everywhere. Take popular culture for example. Catholics definitely hear the word of God in divinely inspired Scriptures. But we can find the word of God in a comic strip, too, or in a novel by Charles Dickens or George Eliot (Mary Ann Evans) or by Stephen King or Ann Tyler.

With her engaging, lively style Mary Kavanagh Sherry whistles up the great mystery of what it means in everyday, sacred terms to experience life as a Catholic in today's uncertain, knockabout, wonderful world. She writes of mysteries and manners, finding and losing, joy and sorrow, and the deep-down peace that comes when you plumb the depths of the Catholic faith. Read on, read on, and let her words settle in your bones. Believe me, thrice blessed will you be, and seventy times seven times will you want to give copies of this book to all your friends.

*—Mitch Finley*

# Introduction

WHAT is a "real" Catholic? Well, I suppose that could depend on one's point of view.

- If you are a practicing Catholic but feeling out-of-sync, a "real" Catholic might be the super-devout person in the next pew. You know the one: so focused, never missing a response, and—if that weren't intimidating enough—her kids behave.

- You may be a baptized Catholic, but not practicing the faith. Then for you, a "real" Catholic might be your co-worker, who shows up on Ash Wednesday with ashes. He hasn't a clue that he makes you a bit uncomfortable, the ashes reminding you of the days when it was effortless for you to be a "real" Catholic. Or maybe your discomfort springs from the fact that the effort proved so difficult that it drove you away.

- You could be a practicing Catholic, but stalled, having been there, done that. You have a vast collection of T-shirts from Cursillo, Marriage Encounter, Retreats-Here-and-There, but you somehow feel disconnected from today's "real" Catholics. They are too conservative, too liberal, too. . . .

- Perhaps you are a member of another faith or profess no faith at all, but wondering how a "real" Catholic thinks about things like confession, fasting, daily Mass and other practices that seem, well, unusual—to say the least.

When the essay, "True Confession," (see page 18) appeared in *America,* an amazing number of people said to me, "That is *just* the way I feel about confession!" Some friends belonging to other faiths remarked that now they could begin to understand how Catholics felt when they confessed their sins to another person. I realized the experience I had described was that of a "real" Catholic, real not because I had the answers, but because my experience was one of questioning: "Why do I do this stuff?" or "Why *don't* I do this stuff?" And this questioning, challenging, of oneself is indeed the experience of so very many, and very real Catholics.

I started to explore further, taking on such "givens" as fasting and contributing money to my parish. When Emilie Cerar called and asked if I might consider a book, I was surprised, a bit intimidated, and yet challenged, because she made me think it might be possible. With her encouragement, I began to look at many other areas in the practice of Catholicism that need constant exploration and reflection if they are to keep us spiritually vital. After all, that was their original purpose!

Spiritual vitality is critical for each of us, but ultimately spiritual vitality is the product of the everyday reasoning and struggle that leads one up to the brink. This is the point where you must either come to a screeching halt or make a leap of faith into the arms of the Unknowable and trust that you will be caught safely—that you won't be left to crash and burn.

When I reflect on my "real" Catholic life, I see a pattern. For extended periods I seem to pace back and forth along that brink without taking any risks. Then there comes a stretch when I find myself constantly airborne. Sometimes I balk simply out of fear, hardness of heart or other paralyzing condition. Other times I'm too lazy to deal seriously with doubt, and so I push it into a comfortable background. But when I am willing to struggle, surprisingly, help is there when I need it. It arrives in a late night phone call from a friend a half a continent away. It speaks to me through a priest in the confessional. It is a conversation overheard in an airport. It is a speeding, flashy red convertible that makes me scramble for the curb.

Yet somehow the struggle is amusing. Really! Humor is an ongoing theme in my spiritual life. If you think that seems ridiculous, you need to know about my Uncle Frank. When the altar rail was removed from his parish church, he took it and stored it in his basement, certain that better days would return. But one day, as I told that story, I saw I was turning into a postmodern Vatican II version of him. Another absurdity popped up when I became convinced that my negative feelings about fasting were NOT MY FAULT, but the fault of the bishop of South Bend/Ft. Wayne, Indiana. Silly? Maybe it seems that way to some, but I guess I take my faith so seriously that I manage to see something funny—even incongruous—in it at times.

Another running theme is surrender. One can't struggle forever. Well, let me correct that. One can, and one should struggle, but the struggle should be, in the long run, a progressive thing. Surrender makes the struggle productive and progress possible. When I surrendered and returned to individual confession, an amazing outpouring of grace, challenges, and yes, even new temptations followed. It took some time, a patient confessor, and, again, a sense of humor, but I could see I *was* moving forward! Surrender helps me realize what is important, and it reminds me Who is in charge.

There is more to the practice of our faith than what appears on the surface. But to dive deeper we need to probe our doubts, question our reflexive thinking, and discuss these things with one another. We need to ask: *How important is it for us to remain Catholic? What strategies do we employ to do so?*

Questions like these can't be answered unless we disengage our "auto-pilot" and get an intellectual grip on our faith. In his sermon, "The Travesty of Truth," Msgr. Ronald A. Knox explains why. "The Catholic religion is very much more than a creed; it is a life, a loyalty, a romance. But it is a creed, too; and the assertion of it involves us in an intellectual responsibility. Man's intellect is part of himself, and must be represented, consequently, in the scheme of his salvation."

It is my hope to contribute to this scheme with this book.

# Part I

# *Growing Up Catholic*

# ❊ True Confession ❊

It was a dark and stormy night. It was. Really! I parked in the lower lot and came through the parish center entrance. Taking the stairs two at a time because I was on the edge of being late, I hurried toward the church, thinking about all the *other* things I needed to do before Christmas. The communal penance service would be one more thing I could soon check off my list.

I negotiated the corners and headed into the stretch. As I passed a room on my left, I noticed a piece of paper taped near the door that noted, "Vesting room for priests for the penance service." The room was packed full of priests, vested in albs and stoles. When I saw the sheer number in there, I knew I was in trouble. Deep trouble. It was clear to me what kind of "penance service" this was going to be. . . . I recalled the parish bulletin said "individual confession," but I had assumed it would be an option. I must not have read the fine print.

At this point it would have been fairly simple to hang a left in the atrium and melt into the darkness through the north doors. But I decided to, well, stick it out—at least for a while. I would just pray with the congregation and hope for a general absolution.

I slid into a pew toward the back.

The priests came in and sat in a large group in the pews to the left of the sanctuary. They were young, old, middle-aged. There were even a couple of red beanies—bishops? Really! Hmmm. This was getting interesting. Father Peter, our associate pastor, approached the altar and explained this penance service would not feature general absolution, only individual confession. After a brief Liturgy of the Word, the priests would be stationed throughout the church and atrium. Then he introduced each confessor to the congregation.

I started to rethink my plans. How long had it been since my last individual confession? Even my attendance at communal penance services with general absolution had dropped off. The last one I attended had been at least a couple of years ago. You know how these things get away from you. . . . But individual confession? Let me think. Five years? More like ten. Let's see, when did our kids reach driving age so they could (presumably) go on their own? Good grief! Could it have been *that* long?

Why did I stop going to individual confession? The short answer is I never really knew how to be a good penitent. And, when I matured and made some admittedly feeble attempts to grow into this sacrament, I couldn't seem to find a priest who knew how to hear my confessions to my satisfaction. Over many years, I did find one, but then we moved away, and frankly I didn't search too hard to find another confessor. As soon as penance services with general absolution became a fairly common practice, that worked for me!

It was getting near crunch time. The Scripture had been read, the priests were dispatched to their stations, and the confessionals were open for business.

I sat.

Finally I decided I could . . . I should . . . do this. Now. The atmosphere was inspiring. The people around me were prayerful. The priests within my view were absorbed in what the penitents were saying. The next question was, did I want to go to a bishop? How about a really old priest—one who truly had heard everything there was to hear? Maybe a young priest, who could benefit from my adding to his portfolio. This was getting too complicated. Afraid my resolve would weaken, I just found the longest line and made sure I would be last.

As the line inched forward I started to think about what I was going to say. After all, it had been close to twenty years. The "laundry list" wouldn't work here. I decided to focus on a few points that had been troubling me and see where that led.

Just as I had mentally rehearsed almost to the point of readiness, Father Will, our former associate, strode up to me and said, "I'll hear your confession if you'd like." Oh, no! He *knows* me, not well, but I am not anonymous. This confession will definitely be face-to-face. It was too late to be anything else. It was an offer I couldn't gracefully refuse. Father Will led the way to the atrium where we sat across from one another. I told him about how long it had been since my last general absolution and individual confession, and he didn't blink. Then I told him how I had picked out a few things I felt I needed to talk about. He listened. He gave me some truly useful, pertinent suggestions in each area of my concern. Then he gave me absolution.

Afterwards we talked about this penance service. He told me it had been a powerful experience for him because most people were like me—it had been years since they had been inside a confessional. As we returned to the church, we chatted casually about his new job.

Recently, in a homily, our pastor, Father Jim, said people tell him they don't seem to commit many sins anymore.

I must confess (to you), I don't remember what he said next because I began thinking how I had felt that way too. (I lead a hum-drum life.) However, since my return to regular one-on-one confession, I have been led to introspection and discovery of my own systemic sin. The sacrament has given me an ongoing resource for insight, healing, and forgiveness in this area.

While I have changed my outlook toward the sacrament of reconciliation, it seems to me the mechanics of the sacrament have changed even more. Priests these days strike me as better trained for hearing confessions. They strive to help penitents explore, discover and understand the *why* as well as the *what* of our sin. This is the path to true spiritual growth.

The practice of receiving this sacrament devotionally— that is, confessing regularly when one is not in the state of serious sin—somehow fell through the cracks following Vatican II. Perhaps that wasn't all bad. The hiatus turned out to be an opportunity for confessors and penitents alike to rethink the sacrament and its purpose.

If we seem to be hearing a lot these days about the merits of individual confession, it is simply because of this: reconciliation is a sacrament that can bring the light of grace and calming peace to our dark and stormy nights.

# Daily Mass? Only for the Holy?

Near the end of my senior year in college, shortly after becoming engaged to be married, I was running to a class when I spotted a nun whom I knew slightly. I giddily flashed my diamond, "Sister! Look!" I thought she'd be thrilled to share my joy. Instead, she was visibly shocked. She stammered, "But, but, we thought. . . ." Then, recovering her composure, she said with genuine warmth. "I'm so happy for you, dear. When is your wedding date?"

No telling what people might think when you go to daily Mass.

I've been a daily Mass-er for nearly as long as I can remember. During summer visits with my grandmother, I loved going to 6:30 a.m. Mass with her. Accompanying Nana didn't earn special attention or rewards, nor did it merit "quality time" conversations on the short walk between her house and the church. Nana mostly hummed the entire way. (Just as a matter of record, Nana hummed *all* the time.) We would settle in the first pew to the right of the center aisle and kneel on wooden, unpadded kneelers. My chin barely reached the ledge where Nana would rest her elbows. I liked the smell of the church—beeswax, furniture polish and traces of incense, aroused from dark corners and blended by the faint breeze which portended a sweltering day. I was not yet old enough to go to Communion.

When I was a little older I "played Mass." That was one of those rainy-day pastimes of our day. My sisters and I would set up an elaborate altar, argue over who got to be the priest last time, and "priest," "servers," and lowly congregants alike would murmur "prayers" in "Latin." I don't remember my parents' reaction to the game, but when we were at loose ends and looking for something to do, I doubt they ever said, "Why don't you all go downstairs and play 'Mass?'" Yet there must have been at least some parental oversight because lighted candles were not allowed.

Just about anything else was. We made up our own rules, taking care to include a gospel (or two), a sermon (usually about being kind to one's sisters), consecration and Communion (pass the Necco wafers). We played Mass with the same enthusiasm, adventure, and immersion in fantasy we employed when playing cowboys and Indians, and both games had about equal measures of holiness.

We lived close to our parish church, and as a family of girls, the Kavanaghs were called upon frequently to help out with what we would now consider "women's work." We polished candlesticks, washed cruets and helped the nuns clean the sanctuary, which meant a biannual, exhilarating climb on the huge altar to wipe down the angels and saints that occupied the many niches towering above the floor. The tricky part, as we traversed the altar, was genuflecting on the ledge in front of the tabernacle without falling off. Even the altar boys didn't get to do that, and we could sense their envy if they happened to be practicing for a Solemn High Mass when we were doing our lofty dusting.

For several summers a friend and I served as sacristans when the nuns were away, laying out each afternoon a set of vestments in the reverse order in which they would be donned for Mass the next morning. *"Remember, girls, amice on top and make a nice "M" (for the Blessed Mother) with the cincture."* We learned to read the Latin liturgical calendar so we knew what color chasuble to put out, and—if there were a choice—lay out two, always hoping Father would select the white or the red instead of the boring, repetitive ordinary-time green.

I frequently knew the selection Father made because one of my other jobs was playing the organ and singing for daily Mass. I rotated this duty with my younger sister and another girl, who was much older. Both Anne and Barbara were much better singers and organists than I. Their repertoires included more than Gregorian Chant Mass VIII, IX and XI; and the fact that I kept my job was proof that if there weren't any more talent in the pool, reliability would do.

One would think all this exposure would make a person O.D. on Church, yet it seemed to have an opposite effect on me. It was a comfortable place to be, and probably from about the sixth grade on, even when I wasn't on "duty," I began to drop in for weekday Mass, just because I wanted to. It seemed natural to be there.

Even after I enrolled at the public high school, every so often I got up early for daily Mass, especially in Lent. It seemed unavoidable during college, when all I had to do was walk down a long hall in the dormitory to the chapel. It was a treat when my children were small, and I managed to escape for a day of child-free shopping or museum prowling, starting off with morning Mass. When my life changed again, and I traveled a bit in my work, staying in luxury hotels and living on an expense account, there was nothing like daily Mass for a reality check.

Few others found this habit "natural," however. When friends casually asked how I had spent my day, I usually omitted the Mass part. You get funny looks when you mention that. People tend to infer way too much meaning, specifically, "holiness," from the fact that you usually start or end your day with Mass. This has been a lifelong cross I've had to bear. Many people leap to the conclusion that the young who attend Mass on a weekday are headed for the priesthood or the convent, as did the nun who was surprised to see my engagement ring. In mid-life, daily Mass-ers are assumed to be mortally ill, or related to someone who is. If not, they are between jobs, having trouble with a spouse or frantic over an errant child. When there is no other "good" reason for showing up regularly for Mass, well, you are open to suspicion of being just too "holy."

Then, God save you if, outside of church, you don't live up to others' expectations of daily-Mass-quality-holiness. People wonder out loud to one another: *How can she go to daily Mass and still* behave *that way?* Evelyn Waugh, noted for his prickly disposition, suggested it was only his attendance at daily Mass that kept him from behaving any *worse!*

There are a lot of us who suffer from the effects of such misapprehension. But I know most of the people I see each morning are at Mass for the same reason I go: not because we are holy, but because we know we are needy. What do I *need* to hear today? I have no idea when I set out. But I have confidence that something in the penitential rite, the readings, or the Eucharistic prayer will speak to me and my need that day. And, at the end of the day, I can look back and see that my need was in some way met.

That is only a small part of the sacred, the gift and the mystery that draws me there. Holy Mass is the only prayer that gives me *physical proof* of God's abundance and loving generosity. That abundance will exceed all my offerings of the day. And by its excess it will make mine a little better.

# ❋ Hail Mary and All That ❋

Our family had a special regard for the Rosary. "Special" in that most of us regarded it as an instrument of torture. My grandmother helped form that impression. Literally. She expected all her visitors—even her daughters' suitors—to fall to their knees on the deeply embossed linoleum floor after dinner for the Rosary. As visiting grandchildren, we were required to stay there without squirming for at least 20 minutes, and take turns leading and announcing the mysteries—the deepest of which was why we were doing this in the first place.

My mother carried on the tradition with certain modifications. For one thing, she let us kneel on carpet. She also let us lean on things, like the second shelf of a bookcase where I regularly prayed into the spines of the Complete Encyclopaedia Britannica. (At Nana's—it seemed to me—adult men were allowed to alternate knees and rest their heads on their hands supported by their elbows, while women and children had to kneel up straight and look reverent at all times.)

Mother's approach was radically different from Nana's in other ways, too. Mother rounded us up for the Rosary only during May and October, traditionally months devoted to the Blessed Virgin. Our boyfriends were exempt. And she never let my father's absence, due to some meeting or important business back at his office, be interpreted as a lack of enthusiasm. Mother hoped to make us *want* to say the Rosary. She understood the need for a right intention for prayer and made this point with her annual Rosary joke. At dawn on Christmas, when all seven of us kids gathered at the top of the stairs, waiting for the signal to race down to the living room to see what Santa Claus had delivered, Mother would say, "Before we go downstairs, we should say the Rosary." She was kidding. I think.

However, even with Mother's less stringent approach, the 20-minute exercise always was a forced march through thickets of Hail Mary's and Our Father's and Glory Be's. And I never felt it reached its destination.

I couldn't wait to stop having to say the Rosary. And I did as soon as I left home for college—Rosary College. (Would I ever escape?) The school was run by Dominican sisters, members of the Congregation of the Most Holy Rosary, who, in those days had gigantic, complete, 15-decade rosaries hanging from their belts. All over campus there were paintings and statues of St. Dominic's vision of the Blessed Virgin handing him a rosary, which, as I have since learned, was most likely added by a fervent graffiti artist after the original was painted. For a brief time, after Rosary College went co-ed, the men's basketball team was nicknamed The Beads, and the women cheerleaders were known as The Five Joyful Mysteries. You couldn't miss the theme.

If I received a rosary when I made my First Communion, as most Catholic kids do, I don't remember it. In fact, the only rosary I remember treasuring is one my husband gave me after we were engaged. He must have thought I was a typically pious Catholic girl of our era, and a rosary would be a wonderful gift. Well, it was, and though I wasn't, I must admit that while I didn't say it all that much unless there was some desperate, near-term need, I appreciated its crystalline beauty. I felt sick when I chipped a bead in the middle decade and despaired when I lost it. When the finder who responded to my ad in the paper clearly expected a monetary reward, I was quite miffed— after all this was something *sacred.*. Yet I anted up, somewhat grudgingly. I lost it again in a hotel in Kansas City, this time for good. And I never told my husband. Since I didn't use it very often, he must not have missed it.

Several years ago when a group of us were swapping pre-Vatican II Marian-devotions-run-amok war stories, I made some crack about not saying the Rosary any more. One of our group, a priest who was exceptionally liturgically *au currant,* remarked, "The Rosary is a very difficult prayer." Since he, too, had groused about that era's frenzied excessiveness, he got my attention. I had never looked on the Rosary that way. Tedious prayer? Yes. Boring prayer? Definitely! Pointless prayer? Well, it sometimes seemed that way. Difficult? Now there's a thought—a thought that lurked in the back of my mind for years.

★ ★ ★

"I just know it's malignant," my friend M.C. whispered over the phone. And it was. There wasn't much I could do. We live 400 miles apart. But, I instinctively reached for (now-where-is-it?) a rosary. Out of the dozens left by my late mother-and father-in-law, I latched onto a well-worn simple black one and started first by saying one decade. That was all I could manage without wondering by the sixth Hail Mary if I had taken something out of the freezer for dinner.

My prayer was a desperate pleading for the life of my friend. But the good intention wasn't enough. The repetitiveness drove me mad. My mind went back to what Father Jerry had said years ago: ". . . a difficult prayer." I was grown up now. I had voluntarily picked up the beads. I *wanted* to pray (are you reading this, Mom?) the Rosary because I knew M.C. had great devotion to the Blessed Mother. I would do this for my friend. But to do it right, I had to, well, *think* about it—or completely forget it and resort to another kind of prayer. Furthermore, I had to ask myself if I was simply clutching the rosary as a devotional security blanket, as comforting as my mother's noodles and pork roast. Was this prayer? Could it be *my* prayer?

I wish I could say the answer came to me like St. Dominic's (enhanced?) vision of Our Lady handing him a set of rosary beads, but it came to me in bits and pieces. From saying one decade, I gradually moved on to two decades in one session. Then three, until I got to five. Somewhere in the process I discovered that the secret to any prayer is to start by praying for the desire to pray. Once I took this approach, the Rosary became a tool, a reflection, a portal. . . . Exactly how and why I reached this point is a mystery—at once Sorrowful, Joyful and Glorious.

But the most important discovery of all was that my little rebellion had value. It gave me the space I needed to develop some objectivity about this private devotion that has endured for more than 800 years, in one application or another. The rebellion freed me from having to say the Rosary Nana's way, my mother's way or anyone else's way. It freed me from feeling I had to say it at all. Even now, when I pray the Rosary with a group—who may find it soothing and comforting, I'm driven to distraction.

An individual's religious rebellion is an invitation to view an issue objectively. Yet it is also a spiritual challenge, and that's an important point I had missed. I had to examine my rebellion and discover its roots, test its validity and deal with the result. When we fail at any one of these steps, our rebellion stays rooted in emotional, reactive and immature thinking. Unexamined rebellion gets reduced to a habit, a thoughtless habit, one you can stay stuck in unless you are lucky and something or someone gets your attention and nudges you to . . . well, get a life—a religious one.

The need of one friend, linked to my recollection of the chance remark of another, helped me identify my problems with the Rosary. Funny how that worked. The symbolism of the linked rosary beads as a chain of prayer is inescapable. M.C.'s physical health was restored. And I'm feeling more spiritually connected than ever before.

# ❀ *Saints Be (Ap)Praised!* ❀

Old St. Anne's Church was a place you didn't want to wander into in the dark. Life-size statues of saints—some familiar, some obscure—loomed in the sanctuary. Others attended the side altars, and still more stood in the aisles because there wasn't room anywhere else. If you got there for early morning Mass before all the lights were turned on, St. Anne's was downright spooky! During the last two weeks of Lent, when all the statues in Catholic churches used to be covered with purple shrouds, the place could be terrifying.

On Sundays our family usually sat in a pew near St. Jude, a stern fellow with a strange growth erupting from the top of the his head. (I was nearly out of high school before I realized it represented a tongue of fire.) St. Francis of Assisi had stigmata that made you stare—or avert your eyes, depending on your age, your disposition and your constitution. There were other, less spectacular statues (at least from a child's perspective), but all—especially those parked in the aisles—were worthy of note, if for no other reason than they made the return trip from receiving Communion definitely a heads-up operation.

When a new pastor came to replace the man who had been there for decades, this Confusion of Saints gradually thinned. When the old church was razed and a new, "modern" one built a couple of miles away, the remaining statues never made the trip. The spare look was not just the will of the new pastor. Statues and paintings were vanishing from other church buildings. The liturgical calendar dropped saints like social undesirables from a guest list. Some saints like Christopher even lost their canonical standing. (But not their constituency. When St. Christopher was decommissioned, my mother-in-law refused to drive her car for weeks.) Those who knew the different levels of ritual for celebrating saints' feast day Masses—simple, double, greater double, double-second class—became an endangered species, whom no one seemed to want to save from extinction. The Roman Missal was shrunk down to a Roman Missalette. This was Vatican II colliding with an old, established culture.

Right about the time St. Anne's got its new look, I went off to a Catholic college where there weren't many statues around, but I was introduced to a new way of venerating the saints. Typed and hand-copied prayers to saints mysteriously and frequently appeared in the chapel pews. They were like pages torn from a catalog of spiritual, physical and social wants. Just pick the right saint, place your order, and your favor will be granted (as long as you make twenty copies of this prayer and leave them for others). I can't remember who could get you a date for Saturday, but I prayed often to that saint. I had better luck with St. Thomas Aquinas, patron of scholars. St. Jude we kept in reserve for hopeless cases in both categories. Even though the sisters would confiscate these scraps of paper and set us straight about superstition, somehow it seemed sacrilegious to throw stuff like that away.

Years later, well after I thought we had become a more mature Church that had outgrown these kinds of devotion, my husband and I were moving to another city and having a tough time selling our house. A very earnest, pious and (as I found out later) *serious* woman told me to bury a St. Joseph statue by the front porch stairs. Since then I have endured listening to otherwise smart people argue passionately about whether St. Joseph should be buried head up or head down, near the front stairs or close to the curb. Not long ago an acquaintance asked if I knew where he could get a really, really big statue of St. Joseph because he had a really, really *big* industrial building to sell. . . .

I would take the St. Joseph statue-as-real-estate-transaction-facilitator as a fluke, but chain prayers seem to be coming back as well. They arrive electronically these days. Well-meaning friends drop them into my e-mail in-box with discouraging regularity. Yet why do I twinge when I send one to trash without winging it on to my entire address book? Do I think bad things will befall me? (There! I've said it!)

It seems we haven't come very far in our view of saints. Our understanding has never matured. We cling safely to the Tradition without probing its underlying Truth. We keep focusing on the miracles and not on the lives. We concentrate on the stories that wear well—heroic deeds and martyrdom that ignite our sense of childlike wonder. But unless we take that wonder to a deeper level, the wonder turns from childlike to childish, and that's not particularly wonderful. The result is a sort of sacred celebrity culture—in which we trade miracle-statistics: lifetime healing average and perfect days lived.

The Church in her wisdom requires miracles as part of the canonization process. A miracle is the popular *pièce de résistance* in proving these people are worthy of inclusion in The Church's canon. Miracles are thrilling, but it seems to me they can dazzle us blind to the saints' relationships with God. During the canonization process, less public attention is paid to the more detailed and deeply explored proof of a life of heroic virtue. Without this component, saints are merely cartoons, empty line drawings an artist makes before filling in color and nuances of expression. Understanding saints' heroic virtue in the context of their times and culture takes work, a lot more work than accepting miracles. But our work doesn't stop there. We are further challenged to translate their heroic virtue into the context of our own culture and time, and—the hard part— practice it. This is how, generation after generation, the saints call us to our own saintliness. But let's face it, generation after generation, it is easier to simply beg for more flashy miracles.

Recently a friend, not a Catholic, asked me if I had a favorite saint. As I confessed I did not, I had the vague feeling I was betraying my faith. After all there is something so very Catholic about saints and our devotion to them. As we talked further, it was clear she had the impression Catholics worshiped saints like minor deities. I told her the relationship was one of asking your friend to pray for you—a friend who is very close to God. If I believe this, I must cultivate this friendship. I need to go beyond praying before statues or paintings and distributing prayer leaflets. I need to read what the saints wrote and understand the times in which they lived. When I do this, I can indeed come back from receiving Communion, bump into one and say, "Join us, friend! You can help me walk with Him for a little way . . ."

# ❄ *S't'r! S't'r!* ❄

I spent most of seventh grade in bed because I didn't like Sister Everilda. We clashed early in the school year over a mysterious property of Zero. Well, "clashed" is a bit strong, because one didn't dare confront any nun in those days, particularly Sister Everilda. Excited about my "remarkable" discovery, I wanted to take her math lesson to new heights. She didn't want to go there. She brushed me off. So I went to bed, and stayed there pretty much until eighth grade.

Sister Everilda did not run true to the type of sisters who had taught me up to that point. She wasn't warm and fuzzy. The girls did not run up to her on the school playground and compete to clasp her hands while clamoring, "Sister, Sis'tr, S't'r! S't'r!" She wasn't feared, but she wasn't particularly liked, either. No nonsense, she would never have been a character in *Nunsense*. Yet every kid in St. Mary's school knew, probably from fourth grade on, that your life's work was to be prepared for seventh grade. And passing seventh grade would mean you were ready for at least sophomore year in the town's public high school.

I should have loved a teacher like that, and she should have loved me. I was a reasonably good student who was born with a finely tuned sense of when to help a teacher out. When Sister asked a question and no one would volunteer, I was willing to make a stab at it, knowing my answer—correct or not—filled an awkward moment. (Teachers appreciate that. I know. I've taught.) But I wasn't filling an awkward moment when I shared my deep thoughts about Zero, and there was something in the way Sister Everilda looked at me that sent me off to pout for a year.

Of course, years later, I could see Sister's side. She had forty-some kids in the class. She was determined that we all would read at high school level and have an eighth grade grounding in math by the time she was finished with us. Indulging the whim of a single student was out of the question.

Sister Everilda was my first grown-up teacher. She didn't charm, yet she didn't bark. Her expectations were high, and she made them very clear. No one was excused. No one was favored. As far as she was concerned, my interest in Zero may have been quite fascinating, but I could go off and contemplate it to my heart's content—by myself. That I did not was my failure, not hers. On further reflection, I see she was like a good mother, looking out for the welfare of *all* her children, not just one or two who showed a spark of promise.

These days, it's common to be a bit more reflective about the Sister Everildas in our own lives, our relationships with them, and the contributions teaching nuns made to our personal lives and the broader culture. In the 1970s and 1980s we found hilarity in books and films that openly mocked nuns and what they taught. What silly notions they had about sex! Abstinence until marriage? Gimme a break! Modesty? How medieval! Manners and respect for authority and elders? Unbearably elitist!

Today, nuns continue to fascinate us, but something has changed. While they are still parodied in popular literature and entertainment, the tone has turned nostalgic. Could we simply be getting older and remembering the good old days as they never were, or are we merely growing wiser and perceiving the value in something we rebelled against? Like our mothers.

While Sister Everilda was the mother who looked out for all her children, a mother driven to raise them to excellence as a group, there were other sister-mothers I had who helped me learn who I am and led me to see what I could become. There were practical mothers who made the convincing argument that proper comportment (now, *there's* a good nunnie term!) and good English would open doors for us no matter what our family background. There were intellectual mothers who prepared us for real-world challenges to our faith. One of these, in a departure from our textbook, made a big deal of the theory of evolution. She flew around the classroom, hammering the point that this was a theory, and that it was not incompatible with our belief that human souls are created by God. "I just wanted you to know that," she concluded in a somber tone, "before you get to the public high school."

There were fun mothers, who played baseball and jumped rope expertly and celebrated St. Patrick's Day and other feasts with a joyous abandon. A particular favorite of all, Sister Catherine, suddenly (and mysteriously, given she was only a grade school music teacher) appeared one day at the college I attended. She and I sat up all night talking (I talked; she listened) about a serious faith crisis I was in. She disappeared the next day, leaving in her wake advice I have repeated to those similarly troubled.

There were crabby, short-tempered mothers. There were mothers who favored the boys, and some who favored the girls. But sooner or later you got the mother you wanted, or needed, or deserved. . . .

For a couple of generations we blamed a lot of our problems on these mothers. As we whined about our dysfunction, we failed to recognize that they gave us a value system in which to function. We took for granted that we were able to express our complaints with perfect grammar and flawless syntax. Yet as I observed a moment ago, we seem to be entering a new phase. Are we, at last, looking past the individuals and seeing worth in the values they gave us? With all our loose talk about the values we want for our own children and grandchildren, have we finally seen these are the same values the sisters helped form in us? We are uneasy, however, because we know as we teach these values within our households, we need reinforcements on the outside. But where are the mothers?

When we let on that teaching seventh grade was an "unworthy" mission, lots of sisters left. Many kept their vows but went on to jobs that had more . . . well . . . respect. I wish I could say that the vowed women religious simply had gone to bed to pout until we "got over it." But that certainly is not the case. The Sister Everildas of this world eventually retired. Many died. And few are stepping up to take their place. Our culture doesn't see nurturing jobs as valuable, worthy vocations, so it shouldn't surprise us that women's religious orders no longer see them that way, either.

The lack of nurturing is taking its toll on our culture, and it is affecting our Church. I think it shows. . . . We would get low marks on comportment, to mention only one category. However, even if we tried to remedy that by crying out, "S't'r! S't'r! and reach out, hoping to clasp a hand, none is there.

Vatican II: Let It Be . . . Let It Be

After a huge fight with Father Bernard, his cousin, Uncle Frank brought the altar rail home and stacked it in his basement. As Father Bernard's major donor, and his primary critic, Uncle Frank thought Vatican II was a complete mistake. But Father Bernard had his orders (the kind a pastor gets from his boss), and bishops trump cousins, even the ones that give the big bucks. The altar rail had to go.

This was in the early 1970s, and I just couldn't understand why Uncle Frank didn't get it. Suddenly being a Catholic was "in;" it was fun! We were overbooked with home Masses, the underground Church and floating parishes. We formed parish councils and rose out of the pews to be Eucharistic ministers and lectors. We organized religious education programs to teach our children about God's love instead of God's punishment. We breathlessly co-created a new era in the Church: Beyond Bingo! We ditched our Baltimore Catechisms, chapel veils, Gregorian Chant and a lot of other "baggage" in the process.

If you were born after 1962, your eyes are probably glazing over. What's the big deal about an altar rail anyway? (For that matter, what's an altar rail?) And at your tender age, you probably didn't get too worked up either on November 29, 2001, when the news broke that George Harrison had died. Early that morning I flicked on the television, and the two news anchors, uncharacteristically somber, got my attention. Clearly something terrible had happened, and I watched apprehensively. Heads bowed, the anchors listened to a distraught remote reporter, whose name I didn't recognize. At last a crawl identified him as a local disk jockey. Then I got it; one of the Beatles had passed on.

The anchor-*Kinder* were twenty-something. As they became visibly bored with the D.J.'s reminiscing and politely tried to get him to wind up his report, one struggled to suppress a yawn. Suddenly I felt like I was in church. No, not at Mass, but at a lecture or study group, where people of a certain age wax melancholy as they lament the "unravelling" of Vatican II. You know how those sessions go: alarmed concern for the conservatism of our newly ordained priests and the shepherds' attempts to drive us back into the confessional; and groans of angst at the now-clear signs that women are not going to be ordained—maybe ever. And whazzamatter with this generation? No one appreciates how the identity of the pseudonymous Vatican II session reporter, Xavier Rynne, was so long kept secret! Or cares! They don't even recognize the name! Then, someone mentions an absent regular who is in the hospital getting an artificial knee or hip or pacemaker and does glucosamine really work? All the while, the "kids" among us sit politely with frozen smiles, glancing at their watches, and looking for opportunities to escape.

When I reflect on Vatican II and the decade following it, I have to admit those years were immensely fun. They were more than fun; they were rip-roaring good times, fueled by youthful energy, new ideas, and joyful optimism, oh, and a little boundary breaking as well. I recall going to a parish Halloween party dressed as a bishop, bearing a sign that said "Today St. Richard's, Tomorrow Rome!" I chose my costume hoping to get a rise out of Father Tom, one of our associate pastors, whom I considered a bit too conservative on the women's ordination issue. It didn't work. He showed up wearing a nun's habit.

But somehow the good times didn't continue to roll. When it became clear newly elected Pope John Paul II, that cool, *young* pope, was putting the brakes on the direction we thought The Church should be taking, like many others, I became grumpy and out of sorts. It took George Harrison's death to help me figure out what was really going on inside me.

The day George died, I went for a walk with two neighbors. Beth, in deep mourning, described with drawn-out sighs how she and her friends were so caught up in Beatlemania as teenagers. Theirs was unbridled joy, energetic optimism and daring boundary-breaking. Mary Sue, who is ten years younger than Beth, murmured nice things about the Beatles' music in the manner of one offering condolence but unable to relate to the loss. Then Beth observed, "This is really about the passing of my youth." And I agreed.

Youth thrives on change, on innovation, on believing it is breaking boundaries. Age settles into the safety of sameness. "The old ways work for me, and they can and should (and will-by-golly) work for you!" But when I look around The Church Universal, I see coming from the top a hierarchy directing us away from what have become "old ways," even if they have been around for only 30 years or so. I sigh because these are the ways of my youth, the ways of my unbridled joy, my glorious, heady, deliriously fun, boundary-breaking times. However, I have to honestly admit to seeing some diversion from the "old ways" coming from the bottom, too. What am I hearing at Mass these days but Gregorian Chant! Hmmm, I used to love that. . . . How interesting the young music ministers are bringing it back. The Asperges, incense, chasubles? Quaint. But it is the young who pulled them up from the ecclesiastical basement and today find them ceremonial, reverent and relevant.

Recently I was sorting out these thoughts over some Holy Water with Father Ed, a long-time friend, who has been treading Earth little longer than John Paul II. This (among other things) gives him a deeper perspective than mine. He brought me up short by pointing out it took 100 years for the work of the Council of Trent to become fully implemented in the Church. The time lag was not due entirely to communications "technology" of 1545 to 1645. It simply took time, thought and study to address the crucial issue: how to hand off The Church from one generation to another, intact. It was not a new problem then, nor is it now. Both Old Testament and New speak of handing down our faith to succeeding generations. Even our liturgy resounds this theme: "From age to age, You gather a people to Yourself, so that from East to West a perfect offering may be made to the glory of Your Name." While that sentence captured my imagination when I first heard it in English (thank-you-very-much-Vatican II), it is only recently that I have begun to mull over the "age to age" part.

Although nothing works quite the same from age to age, each age tends to think they've gotten it right, at last. Mine certainly did. But each generation wants to skip past the hard part: what fills the needs of one generation does not necessarily—in its exact form—meet the needs of succeeding generations. So to successfully pass something on, we often have to let some parts of it go, recognizing we have been only temporary caretakers. Think about it! Wasn't that what Vatican II was all about anyway?

When Uncle Frank went to his reward he still had high hopes for the resurrection of the altar rail. Before I go to mine, I need to check my basement. Like Uncle Frank's, it's full of treasures webbed in fond memories. Why am I hanging on to music that speaks only to my age group and other symbols that marked *my* era? Am I lacking the grace, confidence and *humility* to trust that my children's generation will receive the grace they need to use the legacy of our faith appropriately, use it for *their* spiritual growth, and thus have a solid inheritance—a true heritage they can pass on to *their* children?

It is much like the Beatles' music: the good stuff will manage to live on. Instead of being loud, rule breaking, and in-your-face, it becomes accepted, ordinary and universal. Today it has a Salsa flavor or perhaps it's heavy with strings. How it came to be may remain in only a few memories, fodder for historians, but when subjected to new interpretation, its essence gets tested and proven good. As the evolution proceeds, we can muse, "Ah! I *know* that tune!" And we can rejoice that the beat goes on.

## *Questions for Reflection and Discussion*

1. Realizing that it is important to you to stay Catholic, what points in Part I speak strongly to you about doing this?

2. Is rebellion necessary for the development of a person's faith? How do you deal with it in yourself? How do you deal with others when you see them in a state of inner religious rebellion?

3. How has your understanding of confession, daily Mass, saying the Rosary or praying to the saints been affected by your reading?

4. Are there any new insights you have in reflecting on an experience with a nun that you or a family member "pouted over" as a young person?

5. Do you think the Church of your youth will be the same Church when your children and grandchildren reach your age? Should it be? How do we personally hand off our faith to the succeeding generation?

6. How can you assist the Church in welcoming and gathering people of every age and from age to age into the Body of Christ?

# Part II

## *Growing Up*

*Offer-It-Up? Oh, Sure . . . Right!*

Whenever I hear someone say, "Offer-it-up," I remember Sally. Sally had a fondness for sweets, but they weren't good for her. Every time she spied me sneaking a cookie or candy bar, she would stare intently at me, hoping I'd feel guilty and share. "Offer-it-up," I would tell her, enjoying my little joke. The basset hound's baleful expression wouldn't change, but she would wiggle the little white tip of her tail. Even if she didn't understand the humor or get the treat, she was happy that at least I acknowledged her presence and her desire.

"Offer-it-up." What a catch-phrase that is! In one swoop it speaks of generations of Catholic culture—handed down from mother-to-child, teacher-to-student, and, according to what I hear from some of my friends, an occasional clueless confessor-to-penitent. I suppose some people who told me to "Offer-it-up" when I was young, sincerely wanted me to learn about a penitential spirit and patient endurance. But I think the intention of most was usually to dismiss, to say: Quit complaining! Get on with your life! The expression was used so frequently and casually that it turned into code, one getting hearty laughs when spoken in the right company.

What is the "it" in "Offer-it-up?" When our mothers said this to us when we were children, the "it" was the small stuff we whined about. Having to share, having to do chores, having to watch over our younger brothers and sisters, were big "its" in those days. If we obeyed our mothers, when we offered these things up, we stopped complaining and performed these tasks with a light heart—or pretended to do so. And Mother was happy.

The scope of "it" broadened when we got to school. The sisters who taught me said we should be offering up our small acts of penance such as kneeling without fidgeting during Stations of the Cross in Lent and the grueling Sorrowful Mother Novena, which we attended each Friday afternoon as a student body. Maybe we were physically uncomfortable (no pads on those kneelers), but we were quiet, and building character. And Sister was happy.

That was about as far as I got in the theological development of "offering-it-up." I had heard—and used—the expression so often by the time I got to high school, "offer-it-up" had already ascended to the level of a joke. If I were dateless for Homecoming, I'd roll my eyes and (in my misery) quip to friends and family that I supposed I would have to "offer-it-up." Dealing with crabby customers during my part-time job was another thing to offer up, as was chauffeuring my younger sisters so I could earn the use of the family car. By fine tuning my application of the phrase, I acquired a clever, socially acceptable way of making sure people knew I was being inconvenienced, disappointed or reluctantly having to make adjustments to my plans. And that made me happy.

Years later, when I was old enough to be implementing my mother's offer-it-up strategies with my own children, I learned the expression could have dark undertones. Occasionally I'd hear about someone who was trapped in a marriage to a raging, chronic alcoholic or drug addict and who was being advised by a confessor to "offer-it-up." And, presumably, because another marriage was "saved," Father Confessor was happy.

I noticed, however, that the "its" kept getting bigger as my life went on. I listened sympathetically to friends who were faced with an unplanned pregnancy, a job loss, a destruction of a home by fire, the death of a child, abandonment by a spouse, chronic illness, physical injury or mental anguish. I stopped saying, "Offer-it-up."

Why? I realized that whether "it" appears low on the scale as small stuff, or at the other end of the scale as life or soul-threatening, the problem with our traditional and reflexive "offer-it-up" approach is the implication that if you offer something up, the mere act of offering will make "it" disappear. And if the trouble doesn't quite disappear, at the very least, the misery accompanying "it" will evaporate. Sally, the basset hound, was my teacher here. She knew the truth. "It" does not go away.

But doesn't *something* happen to "it" when you offer-it-up? I believe it does. I further believe our teachers, parents, religion instructors and priests, failed us by not helping us connect the dots. They taught us to focus only the giving end of the offering. What about the receiving end, God's end?

Any offering is accepted or rejected. It is ignored or admired. It is used or misused. An offering "up" is not made to make our mothers happy, our teachers agreeable, our priests secure or ourselves content. When we look at it this way, we can see the "its" should include all things— large and small. "Its" should be happy events as well as difficult times. The surprise check that arrives in the mail, the chocolate cake a friend spontaneously shares, the early holiday morning quiet when you are suddenly aware there is no highway noise, are "its" that should be offered, too.

Then we are returning to Him all the "its" that make up the whole of life.

The deep, unsolvable mystery is that the meaning of our offering is unknown to us at the moment we make it, and we probably won't know the meaning until after we die. It could be important for the sanctification of our own souls. It could be significant because others take note and then consider their own offerings. There are ways beyond our imaginings that God, though He does not need what we offer, could indeed use "it." But our intention is critical. If we "offer-it-up" in the proper spirit, God acknowledges our presence and our desire to serve Him. Then, like Sally, we can be joyful with genuine simplicity.

# ❋ Fasting? But, It's So . . . Mortifying! ❋

It was while I was baking Christmas cookies in mid-December (Oooh, good, here's another broken one!) that I began to think about Lent. Clearly I was en route to surpassing the average 1.4 pounds we Americans gain during the Christmas holiday season. So, in a perverse sort of way, while munching toward Ordinary Time, I thought about Lent—and its benefits.

I've never been too keen on fasting. This, of course, is not my fault. It is the fault of the Bishop of Ft. Wayne/South Bend, Indiana. When I was in college, loooong ago, fasting daily for the entire season of Lent was required of all Catholics who had reached their twenty-first birthday. Unless you were a Notre Dame man. In those days, N.D. was a guy place, and the students were dispensed from fasting. Now, on the other side of Lake Michigan, we Rosary (now Dominican) College women—having certain knowledge we were put on Earth to save the souls of Notre Dame men—had to fast. We were incensed that the Bishop of Ft. Wayne/South Bend chose to make our mission even more challenging. Besides, it didn't seem fair. Oh, the Archbishop of Chicago dispensed us for St. Patrick's Day, and—if you had connections to the right parishes —St. Joseph's Day, but for 40 days and 40 nights we fasted. Not perkily, I must add.

Following Vatican II, canonical fasting throughout the entire 40 days of Lent, fell out of favor. Suddenly we were supposed to implement a new model. The intent was to guide us to a more mature approach to penance, but the practice took on the secular zeitgeist: self-improvement. We began giving up alcohol, cigarettes, junk food, soda pop. As part of this new model of penance, we were supposed to focus on doing positive actions in the place of old-fashioned denial of food, but "giving up" seemed to be the dominant trait of our practical religious heritage.

Over the years, this has led me to some creative Lents. Once I gave up Talbot's Outlet Store. Two years ago I gave up Day Trading. While mention of these self-denials generally gets smiles and an occasional, "Are you serious?" the contemporary model of Lent has taught me that six weeks is long enough to break a habit. (Just look at my wardrobe and my portfolio.)

But I'm thinking about retro, pre-Vatican II fasting again, and not just because of the Christmas cookies. Well, that's not quite accurate. While baking for the great feast of Christmas, I had the sudden thought that there is something lacking in current Lenten practices. For one thing, they deny us the concept of feast.

Consider the person who gives up alcohol or gambling. He is not likely to go out on a celebratory binge on Easter Sunday. Or, in my own experience, when I gave up Talbot's, I wasn't standing in front of the store waiting for the doors to open on Easter Monday. I found after a six-week "vacation," I had lost interest. This is not to say there is nothing redeeming in the behavior modification kind of fast. There is, if it is done in the right spirit, the one called mortification. Yet even then, you have to admit it misses something when it comes to the feast. Fast/feast. They go together. Yin/yang. One is not really complete without its opposite.

Just for fun, I looked up pre-Vatican II regulations on fasting. (I know, I need a life.) I was mildly surprised to discover there wasn't much discussion of "feast." The burden of measuring (I can remember my grandmother weighing out her food), figuring out when a liquid was nourishment, and fasting under the "absolute norm" vs. "relative norm," were the focal points of the law. (By the way, I came across an interesting piece of trivia. Our present rule to fast on Ash Wednesday and Good Friday was considered the minimum required under the wartime faculty of dispensation that Pope Pius XII gave to bishops of the Latin Rite during World War II. Now *there's* some food for thought . . .)

Anyway, back to the idea of "feast." No, hold that thought for a moment. First let's talk about hunger.

One of our friendly, local, creative-penance-giving confessors told me a few months ago to meditate on the Magnificat. (Just why, is between him and me.) In the translation I have of this passage from Luke's Gospel, there is a line that says, "He has filled the hungry with good things..." What does this mean? The meaning is obvious to those who live from hand to mouth—the vast majority of people in Our Lady's time, and even in our world today. Yet you and I probably never have known what it is like to be truly hungry for food. I, for example, tend to confuse "hunger" with a regular craving for Fritos. But does the fact that we know where our next meal is coming from mean we cannot experience real hunger? Do we have other hungers? What are they? Have we identified them? Confronted them? Quick, name one.

I've been thinking the hunger that comes from fasting from food could serve as a metaphor for that real, spiritual hunger I have—the one that I find so difficult to name. Fasting could be a vehicle for getting my attention so I can see it. Name it. Reach for it. Embrace it.

To have a genuine feast, we must come to it hungry. Otherwise the feast is reduced to a rote ritual—like that of a young couple faced with having to consume two Christmas dinners—one at her folks' and one at his. In the words of the Magnificat, God has filled the hungry with good things, and the "rich he has sent away empty." The "rich" simply weren't "hungry."

As I approach this Lent, I'm not certain how I will observe it penitentially. Am I ready—really, really ready, to fast in the proper spirit for the entire season? As I wrestle with this, I have to focus on the objective: to learn that my hungers, whatever they may be, will be satisfied only by The Feast.

# ✺ Take Our "Bread" ✺

I never really understood stewardship until its true meaning came to me literally as a bolt out of the blue. One night a few years ago, as I lay half-awake, enchanted by the electric blue flashes and sharp, reverberating thunder of a slow-moving thunderstorm, a blinding yellow bolt, with a simultaneous deafening explosion, made me sit straight up in bed. I was sure the house had been hit.

"No, the house is O.K.," my husband murmured, barely raising his head from the pillow. "Go back to sleep." He did. Of course, I couldn't. The dog and I trudged downstairs for a few (separate) bowls of Captain Crunch to calm our nerves and watch for telltale smoke.

The next morning we found the damage. The three of us gazed awestruck at the remains of a huge tree that had stood just outside our bedroom window. It had been blasted to bits. "This is a sign," I whispered. Quickly calculating the odds, I added, "I'll be right back. I'm going to buy a lottery ticket."

That afternoon, with a Powerball ticket in my pocket, I gathered wood-shrapnel from my neighbors' yards and mentally distributed my "sure-as-getting-hit-by-lightning" financial windfall to causes I deemed worthy. My parish's share of this pot would come to about $13 million. Now wouldn't *that* be fun to drop in the collection basket! Hmmm, maybe not. Who, except for the few famously discrete parishioners who count the collection, would ever know of my "generosity?"

That thought was enough to make me yearn for the good old days. When I was quite young and living in another state, our family moved "up" from The South Side to *THE* North Side of our two-parish town. Annually each parish published a list of parishioners and their contributions. (Required reading? No kidding!) We were barely settled in the new house when my dad learned to his amazement that social respectability at St. Anne's (*THE* North Side parish) cost only $3.00* per week, while at St. Pat's (the other parish) social respectability had cost him more: $5.00* per week. (*Note: This was a long time ago!)

Times have changed, and today parishes rarely push social standing as a motivating button for contributors. However, other organizations creatively play on this frailty of human nature. The congregation of nuns who educated me categorizes donors in subtle code: Partners in Justice, Partners in Peace, Partners in Charity, Partners in Truth.)

When I see their annual list of donors, I can never re-member which is trump, but the sisters know I'm going to try!

Well, I knew my parish could use $13 million, and resignedly, I decided I could live with anonymity and no change in my social standing. So as I continued picking up pieces of the shattered tree, I imagined dropping that huge sum into the collection basket, earning a Partnership in Whatever, and doing other "good" with my winnings. I automatically set aside some of the larger chunks of wood for a winter fire. My winnings aside, I was still going to be frugal.

Maybe it was that image of a fire, fused with the fantasy of giving money away, but something prompted me to muse about my earliest lesson in sacrificial giving. It was probably yours, too. Remember the illustration in those old Bible Histories of the smoke from Abel's sacrifice rising to heaven while the smoke from Cain's hugged the ground? It fascinated me then as it does still now, that both Cain and Abel, as well as later generations of our religious forebears, burned up their offerings to God. After all, this was good, usable *stuff!:* vegetables in Cain's case, a lamb in Abel's. Yet they burned them to worthless ashes. Even as a child I saw something so intimate, so immediate, so linking one's livelihood to God in this type of sacrifice, that it made a lasting impression.

It's pretty difficult for me to see my contributions to my parish—cash, a check or equities—having the same intimacy and immediacy between the giver and the Recipient. Sure money is the fruit of my labor (and stuff I can always use), but it's very hard to view it as some*thing* I am offering to God. It occurred to me that the notion of immolation—destruction—holds the key: I don't really abdicate control of my gift; i.e. let it "go up in smoke." I confess that when I put my envelope in the basket as it goes by, I want to . . . well, follow the money. I need to make sure it is used in a way in which I approve. The result is a subtle shift in intention that makes my "offering" merely a donation.

Is there a difference? There are several differences. (You'll need to work with me here. . . )

**Donation:**

- An exchange between equals: man to man.
- Not owed. Totally voluntary.
- Immediate benefit to donor: tax deduction, social standing, sense of power.

- No risk to donor. Comes from existing resources. Thus it is practical.
- Targets a specific need of the recipient.
- Giver can retain some control (designate where it is applied, etc.).
- Intent of donor is of negligible importance.

## Offering:

- An exchange between unequals: man to God.
- Owed. Involuntary.
- No discernible benefit to giver.
- Risky. Comes from existing, plus future or anticipated resources. Thus it is extravagant.
- Recipient has no need.
- Donor has no control of how gift is used. (So in this sense it is "destroyed.")
- Intent of giver is of essential importance.

Now the question is this: which of these, donation or offering, can we unite with the bread and wine used in that Perfected sacrifice and honestly say, "Look with favor on these offerings and accept them as once you accepted the gifts of your servant Abel, the sacrifice of Abraham, our father in faith . . ."?

★ ★ ★

Of course you knew all along I didn't win the Powerball. I didn't even come close. But I tucked the worthless ticket into my checkbook. It is still there. It serves as a reminder when I make out that regular check to my parish that I need to ask myself: Is this an offering? Or is it merely a donation?

# ✺  *Why Stewardship?*  ✺

The letter is pretty much the same every year when it arrives. It is an invitation from our pastor to give generously of my time and talent and treasure (how I love that!) to my parish family.

Family? I've been a parishioner for 25 years, and I have to say we toss that term, "family," around so casually, but whom are we kidding?

In these 25 years, I've been through two pastors, and at least 7 associate pastors. I've seen a lot of turnover in other staff members, too. Familiar faces I've seen week after week at Sunday Mass, have sometimes just disappeared, never to be seen again. There are approximately ten thousand of us in this parish. When I look around before or after Mass (*never* during, of course), there are only a few I know by name. A family? That's a bit of a stretch.

Over the past 25 years my involvement in parish activities has been like the moon. Waxing, becoming full, waning, followed by a period of complete invisibility. There have been years when I've been totally The Church Lady. At such times, I've been full of enthusiasm, caught up in a mission. Other times I have been a virtual lump, only coming to Mass to sit in a back pew and treat the parish as a mere spiritual watering hole. Sometimes I've been grumpy and complaining, too. (Note to self: ask the pastor when those kneelers will be fixed. . . .)

So, when I ask myself why should I give my time and financial support to this parish, rather than somewhere else, my first thoughts are, well, pretty self-centered. I struggle to find the reason. Then I realize the true reason is not about me, but about the people I rub elbows with at Mass on Sunday—every one of them.

These people have given my now adult children their religious education. They prepared them for, and witnessed their marriages. They prayed for our family when my husband was ill and dying. They helped me bury him and mourn him. Even if they weren't involved in the ministries that served me in this way, through their financial offerings, they have heated and cooled this church, making worship comfortable for me. They've turned on the lights. They've plowed the parking lot. They've renovated the parish buildings. Thanks to them, I don't have to dodge buckets collecting rainwater coming through a leaking roof. They've provided gorgeous vestments for our priests. They have made beautiful music, helping make even the most ordinary Masses inspiring and prayerful for me.

And I am grateful to our priests for sharing their gifts of Orders. They've anointed me twice for serious illness. And when I was ready to return to individual confession after a long hiatus, they have been—and continue to be—compassionate and most patient confessors.

All of these things have fostered my spiritual growth over the past 25 years. Yet these are *other* parishioners' offerings—*their* time, *their* talents and *their* money. And, week after week, they have laid these gifts on the altar to be joined with the bread and wine that our priests offer in the most Perfect Offering humankind can make.

So, it seems only right for me to put my offering of time and a share of my finances right there, on our altar alongside their gifts. Because, and there's no getting around it, even if I can't call each member of this congregation by name, we're family.

## Parish Shopping/Parish Hopping

"I'm going out to shop for a parish this afternoon," I told my husband as I dropped him off at his new office. I announced my mission as if I had planned to run over to the mall—a mall where I could look at a selection of parishes, turn them over, feel their fabric, narrow the choice by eliminating certain textures and patterns, choose one, fold it up, throw it in the trunk and haul it home.

We had just signed a contract to buy a house in Burnsville, Minnesota, a place as foreign to us as a country with a name ending in "istan." My husband's job transfer offered us the perfect chance to find the *right* parish this time. Our last parish experience hadn't been particularly ugly, just unsatisfying. We simply felt we needed more. So, arriving in a new town, without friends or family to nudge us in a particular direction, we seized the opportunity to survey the parishscape rather than fall into a pew in the nearest Catholic church.

This adventure would be A First for me. We had always dutifully stayed within parish boundaries. Thoughts that I might ignore these boundaries made me pause, and in truth pumped me up a bit. I was going to do something mildly rebellious! Years back, you couldn't jump parish lines, even if you wanted to. Fellow parishioners would assume you had some very dark reason for not registering in your parish. ("You live *where?* Oh. . . .") Parish membership gave you an identity. It told outsiders in general terms where you lived, determined where you were likely to send your kids to high school, and connected you with people-you-should-know. And then there was that little issue of money. You were expected to support your *local* parish, no matter what, not a parish on the other side of town. Pastors especially liked that part.

I found the closest parish, deciding to begin the elimination process there. A nun very kindly gave me an overview of the parish activities and the liturgical styles at each weekend Mass. When I asked about boundaries, she looked at me askance. "Boundaries? Hmm. Well, where do you live?" I told her where we were moving. "Well, I guess that would be within our official territory, but I'd have to look it up to be certain. We would prefer you join a parish where you feel comfortable. Now, a little bit west of here is St. John's. . . ." *Welcome to Minnesota,* I thought, happily. *This IS a strange place!*

We were content in that parish for the next ten years or so. Then, well, you know how long term relationships can get. Over time tensions develop with Some People Who Seem to Run Everything. A physical expansion plan appears unduly excessive and expensive. One gets to know way too much about parish politics. Little things start to annoy you. You wish there was a different cantor at the 9:00 a.m. Mass. There are too many unruly kids at the 11:00. Mass at 7:30 is just too early. Why don't they have an 8:00? The assistant pastor you liked so much has been transferred. Can't they find some new speakers or come up with some different programming? So, you ask yourself, what's holding us here? After all, the kids are gone . . . we don't have to stick around for sacramental preparation any more.

We decided to shop again.

There was something different about this shopping expedition. We started the venture by going to Sunday Mass at the surrounding parishes. Each seemed nice, yet. . . . Then we found a downtown parish that was urbane, totally kid-free, had great music and preaching, but . . . well . . . the main problem was that it was *totally* kid-free. About once a month we would interrupt our search and drop back into our home parish to support it financially, sort of. We contributed on a diminished scale, feeling obligated to spread our funds among the other parishes we were visiting so regularly.

This was work! We'd hear of a hot parish to the East. Another to the West. And away we'd go. We felt that if we were to make a fair appraisal, we had to repeat our visits. After each excursion, on the drive back from Mass, we spent the entire time critiquing the homily, the presider's style, the congregation's reverence, the music, the lighting, the heating or cooling and did-you-get-a-load-of-those-weird-blue-votive-lights? Finally, one Sunday, after attending Mass some distance away, we were both silent all the way back. I'm not sure if I said it first, or my husband did, but we were of one mind: "Let's go home."

I think it had dawned on both of us that we really weren't parish shopping, we were parish hopping. It was a spiritual version of being unable to sustain a committed relationship. We thought we knew what we were fleeing from, but what were we looking for? Our objective wasn't clear to us because we had never really asked ourselves that question. I think if we had been more introspective, we would have understood earlier—during the Mass—critiquing exercises, for example—that we were perilously close to looking to be entertained.

After we plugged back in, we looked at our parish with new eyes. Yes, the same problems were there, but we realized none was catastrophic, and we could choose to ignore them—or at least not let them distract us. We saw that even if the parish didn't meet our needs with the same pizzazz it had a decade earlier, it indeed met the needs of a lot of people. Therefore, even if we provided only our presence and financial support, we would help support others in their needs. We had focused only on what we saw as our own needs, and thus we were not being open to what we might bring to the rest of the community. "He who is absorbed in his own interests has not yet entered into the Lord's vineyard," wrote St. Gregory the Great in one of his homilies on the Gospels. How well that described us! In effect, each time we visited a parish "vineyard" we were folding our arms, leaning back and saying, "Peel me a grape!"

Is it important to parish shop? There is no question there are spiritual and cultural overtones and undertones existing in parishes that affect our worship. If you plant yourself in a vineyard where you feel you can never take root, you are not likely to bear fruit. If you plant yourself in a place where you sense you can grow, you probably will.

What about parish hopping? Spiritual boredom is real. But it is a problem with internal, not external remedies. When we beat the path to hot parishes with lively liturgies, where do we go when those parishes inevitably cool? How soon before we ask, *Why we should go to Mass if it is dull?* It's a small step beyond that to ask, *Why should we go to Mass unless we really* feel *like praying?* And, the next step, *Why go to Mass? . . . Oh, it's Christmas!*

Well, we did return to our home parish. While it may no longer be THE place to be . . . for us, it is a place to BE.

# Were You There?

As we shared the last bottle of wine we would have in Paris, my husband and I wondered what was going on along the busy street about a half block away from the café where we lingered. A parade had been passing for at least an hour. We speculated it was one of those legendary French workers' strikes. On this gloomy, drizzly, late January day, no one would be parading for amusement. We were scheduled to fly home the next morning, and while a transportation strike would be a lucky break in my view, it would be a disaster in my husband's. (I was in charge of the fun in our marriage. He was in charge of the money.) Thinking we'd better find out if we had to scramble and change our plans, we paid our bill and walked up to see what was happening.

Solemn marchers—young, middle-aged and elderly men and women, and a few teenagers—filled the broad boulevard in a continuous procession. They walked briskly with purpose. None waved at the spectators. And those watching along the sidelines, equally somber, didn't wave at the marchers. Every so often a priest, wearing a *soutane*, walked by. Now and then a nun dressed in a modified habit appeared in the stream. Periodically a tight cluster of marchers passed, carrying a sign or banner with name of a city: Lyon, Marseilles, Toulouse, Strasbourg, Nantes, plus other words we couldn't decode. Frantically I thumbed my French dictionary and found a clue. "This is an anti-abortion march!" I told my husband.

Wave after wave of people passed silently, but we realized that even in their silence, they were challenging the onlookers by seeking eye contact. Some spectators responded by giving a brisk nod, others stared back, motionless. A sixty-ish woman standing at my left softly muttered threatening obscenities. Despite her—or maybe because of her—we suddenly felt it important to do *le nod*.

A small group of young men, weaving their way through the bystanders on our side of the street, approached us and, holding forth clipboards and pens, eagerly asked us something. I explained in my best "French" that we did not speak French (*alors!* proof!) and thus did not understand his question. The leader then asked in American English if we would sign a petition to limit abortion. We told him we were U.S. citizens so our signatures couldn't be useful to him. But he was very persuasive, and I could read well enough to verify the petition was indeed what he said. We signed.

After watching the marchers pass for another hour, we walked back to our hotel to pack. According to the TV news that evening, the parade continued for at least an hour after we left. The march was impressive, no doubt about that, and it was made more so by the fact that most of the women, exquisitely dressed, marched in high heels! High heels!

A year later, with Paris deposited in my memory bank, I read a reminder in our parish bulletin that the annual anti-abortion march in St. Paul was coming up soon. A flood of excuses lapped around the thoughts I had about participating. I had joined the march a few times several years ago, and I knew what it would be like. The weather forecast called for a cloudy, windy day with a high of ten degrees—so what else is new in Minnesota in January? The setting would be quite the opposite from the silent, stylish, dignified march I had seen the year before. A blaring bagpipe recording of "Amazing Grace" would be played over and over and over and over while people, bundled up so only their eyes showed, shuffled up and down the Capitol Mall sidewalks in their oversize snowmobile boots, some praying audibly, others trading recipes for Hot Dish (defined outside of Minnesota as casserole). Strange, no, really *weird* looking people would carry garish photos of torn, bleeding fetuses and posters showing crucifixes framed by "rosaries" made out of tiny footprints representing beads. And *"those"* would be the people the media would interview for the 10:00 p.m. news. Oh, I nearly forgot to mention—each of those interviewed would have six or seven children in tow, at least three of them under five. No, this would *not* be Paris. . . .

But I went. And it was not Paris. It was just as I had expected—freezing cold and grim in every other respect. On my way home, however, I reflected little on the issue of abortion. I thought about the issue of showing up.

Showing up. It is the way we give voice without saying a word. But often we choose to not speak this language, because it is inconvenient, because we really don't care, or because—and this is my most usual excuse—I don't think I can make a difference. Scripture says a lot about show-ing up. There is that parable about the wedding feast, when the guests don't show, and the king is, well, not pleased (Mt: 22:1-14 and Lk 14:15-24). The fact that only one disciple and a few women showed up at the foot of Jesus' cross, is another lesson—a sad one (Jn 19: 25-26). In each case, if more people had shown up, wouldn't these stories have been different?

Choosing to show up when a crowd is expected anyway requires consumption of a strange combo platter of humility and pride. The prideful tidbit is: if I'm only one in a large crowd, no one will miss me. Of course what I am really thinking is that I'm too important to waste my time being anonymous in a group. *Now if I could contribute something unique by my presence, that would be different!* The feast of humility is the realization that I do make a difference even if I don't have anything more to offer than my presence. Sometimes the only difference it makes is what happens inside *me*.

I mulled over my attitude toward "showing up," and realized I could do a better job of it. I could start with the small stuff: faithfully attending meetings without complaint, voting in primaries and off-year elections, going to a neighbor's retirement party, hauling out for Stations of the Cross during Lent, dropping in for coffee with a friend who doesn't get out much and always seems to absorb too much of my time, and being more generous in attending funerals. In other words, whenever I find myself *looking* for excuses, I should take that as a clue that I should probably show up.

Showing up is a gift of self—a gift of time and energy and attention. This gift speaks more eloquently of honor and respect than any gift purchased with a huge sum of money. It's priceless. And it never goes out of style.

# What Power? Whose Glory?

"Is he your father?" The woman smiled benevolently as I coaxed Father Don to take another spoonful of pureed meatloaf. With his huge bony frame randomly folded and tucked into the wheel chair and his head supported by a neck pillow, Father gave no indication he had either heard or understood the question. Maybe he was concentrating on my promise of vanilla ice cream if he would eat a few more spoonfuls of meat. He swallowed; I mopped his chin. When I pulled back the lid on the ice cream cup, the old priest opened his mouth in anticipation like a baby bird.

"No," I explained, "Father Don was the pastor of my parish, and I'm just a friend." Obviously caught by surprise, the woman murmured awkwardly, "How nice. . . ." and turned to speak to a wizened figure sitting nearby.

With the Catholic priesthood under unprecedented scrutiny, and the secular media not only exposing sinful priests, but also marshalling a frontal assault on celibacy, an all-male clergy, and other long held and cherished (by some) traditions of the Roman Catholic Church, I am haunted by that question posed by the visitor to the nursing home: "Is he your father?"

If he isn't my "father," what is Father Don? Indeed, what is any priest to the person-in-the-pew? Healer? Magician? Wizard, shaman, ecclesiastical policeman, witch-doctor? Spiritual social worker? Clerical Lone Ranger? Each of these roles presumes power. Yet, as I contemplate Father Don gobbling ice cream as fast as I can spoon it into his mouth, he seems anything but powerful.

Promising him more ice cream tomorrow, I roll back the years to when Father Don was at his peak. He had been a powerful guy. He was the popular founding pastor of a huge suburban parish and had a large secular following throughout the community. Father's descent into powerlessness was slow and painful to watch—not to mention what it must have been for him to endure. First he stopped preaching. Then he stopped presiding at Mass. Somewhere in that time a co-pastor was appointed to discretely tidy up parish finances and deal with other details that had gotten away from him. But Father Don's physically imposing presence continued to belie what was really happening. He was still a priest. He still had power.

This priestly power continues to have an aura in the nursing home, where the management has loose connections with the Lutheran community and many employees are Muslims from Somalia. Father Don, who may not even remember that he is a priest, receives respect and deference from all. He still has power.

How attracted we are to power! How repelled we are by it! This applies no less to the Roman Catholic priesthood than to any other position of rank, yet the priesthood brings with it a unique set of problems and circumstances. Ask any practicing Catholic what clerical power means to him or her, and you are likely to get an answer shaped by any number of things. We form our opinions from years of Catholic education—or lack of it; personal experience through counseling, confession or other encounter; a comment from the pulpit; or family lore about how Father Schmidt bungled Uncle Joe's funeral in 1943 . . . wasn't-it-something-about-the-incense-Aunt-Edith-would-remember. . . . If we like our priest, we sentimentalize his role. He becomes Bing Crosby in *The Bells of St. Mary's*. If we don't like him, we tell everyone—and then send him the message via the collection basket.

But we, both clerics and laypeople, can forget that priestly power has one source: the sacrament of Orders. Any other power a priest has—particularly the power of personality—has no connection. The conflicted, shy, quiet, unassuming, *Diary-of-a-Country-Priest*-priest has just as much power as a dynamic, brick-and-mortar, self-assured community-organizer priest. We tend to forget this and confuse sacramental with secular powers. Furthermore, when we laypeople assign too much power to a priest, we not only tempt him to assume power that does not belong to him by virtue of Orders, but we subtly abdicate our personal responsibility. Take Pete, who—to this day—is still mad at Father Don for something he said in a homily 30 years ago. Pete has long since moved away, but hasn't been to Mass since. Then there's Margaret who is convinced she will go to Hell if she doesn't say a rosary each and every day because some priest, she can't remember exactly who, when, or why, apparently told her so.

So, if Father Don isn't my "father," what is he? Once, years ago, at a weekday Mass, Father Don asked the six of us who were attending what our view of God was. I said that God was whatever I needed Him to be. And, I guess that is what I could say, not only about Fr. Don, but of any priest—he is whatever I need him to be. As I think about it, that is more than I would expect from my most intimate friends. While I don't believe my priest to be quite as versatile as God, I assume he is on call to be my confessor, spiritual director, advisor in times of family trouble, a broad shoulder on which to dump life's miseries, fixer of troubled marriages. Oh, and I forgot to mention that he will say Mass every day, preach brilliantly, keep the money rolling in to support the parish, and be available for instantaneous anointing should that be needed. Intellectually I accept the fact that each of the 10,000 people in our parish should be able to ask for the same from our priest, and each should find it only reasonable that he intuitively tweak his services to match every unique personality and need. Like most Catholics, I don't expect much.

And, like most Catholics, I pigeon-hole priests into a particular role without ever getting to know them. We typecast one another in an instant, but when it comes to priests, we do it in barely a nanosecond. Upon hearing of an assignment, whether pastor or associate, we spread the word around the parish that the New Father is "a lot of fun," "seems shy," "likes (or dislikes) kids," "acts pompous," "too cool," "stand-offish," "over-friendly," "extremely liberal," or "hopelessly conservative." I'm not sure anyone is subjected to more rapid, relentless, or ruthless scrutiny and quick judgment. Really, though, aren't we just sizing him up to speculate on how he'll use his power?

What do we *do* to these men? It starts when George and Marlene's kid—the same one who put a baseball through Aunt Ginny's picture window and ran and hid—announces he's considering the priesthood. Suddenly we begin giving him the star treatment. During his period of discernment we coddle him like a precocious young athlete with potential to make the pros, fearing he might discern the "wrong" way. After all we need priests, and we wouldn't want to let another vocation slip away. . . . "George and Marlene's boy is considering the priesthood," we say in hushed tones. And, after his ordination, it doesn't hurt to know George and Marlene. They've got a new status and prestige. They've got power.

So that's what this is all about: power. Not so much priests' power as our power. Para-clerical power is something enjoyed by those surrounding priests, and the scramble for it kicks in as soon as the aspirant makes his intention known.

There are lots of paths to para-clerical power, and I've trod a few of them. Feeding Father Don in the nursing home wasn't the only time I fed him. My husband and I entertained him many times, cooking and serving him dinner. We also fed him ideas, opinions, criticism, and, I'm sorry to say, on a particular issue, scorn. We had very clear views on how our parish should be run. And, when I think of it, most of what we had in mind had little or nothing to do with Jesus. Yes, Jesus, that champion of the powerless, who, through His own powerlessness, brought unprecedented power to humankind. . . .

Father Don died a few weeks ago. At his funeral Mass, during the consecration, I recalled that last time I fed him in the nursing home. As I went up to receive Communion, it struck me how many times Father Don had fed me. He fed me, and thousands of others, the Body and Blood of Jesus—food available to us through only the consecrated hands of a priest. That was Power, the power of Orders, and he used it to make sure his family was fed.

The question the nursing-home visitor asked still haunts me. But now I think that when she asked, "Is he your father?" I should have said, simply, "Yes."

# ❀ Dies Irae ❀

*Note to self: tell kids that while there's no imminent need to implement a plan, I want the* Dies Irae *sung at my funeral.* I posted this mental reminder as I sang "I'll Be With You In Apple Blossom Time," while a bereaved family and mourners processed out of church following the priest and the casket-on-wheels.

As a member of our parish's pick-up funeral choir—folks usually available on fairly short notice—I attend a lot of funerals. This isn't my favorite thing to do, but it's something I can do. And isn't comforting those who mourn, a spiritual work of mercy? Whether or not this merits a heavenly reward for me, there is an earthly bonus. In Catholic funerals these days, families of the deceased select meaningful Scripture readings, choose significant music, write and deliver poignant eulogies, bring touching photos, and even present favorite memorabilia alongside the gifts of bread and wine the priest will offer on the altar. Since our parish is huge, and too often anonymous, by the time we segue into "Danny Boy," I feel I've made the new acquaintance of a fellow parishioner—the one in the casket.

*Dies Irae, dies illa:* "That day of wrath, that dreadful day . . ." just wouldn't fit in today's funeral liturgy. But more and more, I really want to belt that one out. Needing to get in touch with this feeling, I dug up an old missal to enlighten my dim memory of how Catholic funerals used to be. Out of the depths arose a distinct thought as I read through the ritual: clearly we needed to lighten up. That entire liturgy was steeped in *memento mori* without any relief. The priest wore black. The mourners wore black. Even the casket was draped with a black pall. The prayers were dark, dire, end-on-end warnings of the price of mankind's sinfulness—our own, as well as that of the deceased. The ritual was boilerplate, without any wiggle-room. There was no call for remembering the uniqueness of the person who died. I could never understand why, after the funeral, all the adults couldn't wait to get out of church and repair to the neighborhood bar. Now, I get it.

How different the mood of the contemporary Catholic funeral rite! The liturgical fashion color is white. We've ditched the dirges. We still sanctify the body with incense near the end of Mass, but the rendition of "May the Angels Lead You Into Paradise" is upbeat. We have lots of personalization—and, I fear, along with it, unbridled presumption.

It seems to me that our funerals today seem to merely surf the mystery of life. They no longer challenge us to probe deep into the question of whether or not we are living our own lives according to God's plan. And that's why I'd like to bring back the *Dies Irae:*

> "The Lord of judgment on his throne,
> Shall every secret thing make known,
> No sin escapes that once was sown."

That used to give us something to think about . . . especially the "secret thing" part.

Self-knowledge—the mystery of who we are, our "secret things," and whether or not we are cooperating with God's plan—is a difficult thing to grasp. But such self-discovery is the ultimate goal of a mature spirituality. Unless we keep working inward toward knowing our true selves, it is all too easy to slide into the presumption that God will welcome us with open arms when we die, no matter what we do during our lifetime.

In his treatise, *On Prayer*, in the chapter provocatively titled, "The Usefulness of Temptation (29:17-19)," Origen offers an intriguing approach to grappling with this mystery. He says the key lies in the temptations we have. "Through temptations they (our gifts and weaknesses) become known. Thereafter we can no longer be ignorant of who we are. We know ourselves and can be aware, if we but cooperate, of our wrongdoings." He goes on to explain that Eve's weakness was present even *before* the serpent approached her (Gen 3:1). Cain's wickedness was in his heart *prior* to his killing his brother (Gen 4:8). He gives more Old Testament examples, finally pointing out that Joseph was virtuous and secure in his continence *prior* to the woman's attempt to seduce him (Gen 39:7).

Origen wasn't talking about funerals, but he was talking about what we should be talking about at funerals: how God knows our weaknesses and our strengths better than we do. And our willful ignorance of these things is not—nor will it be—bliss. We have a duty to know ourselves and examine our behavior in the light of whether or not we are cooperating with, or resisting God's grace, before it's too late.

It is no accident that Catholics celebrate the mystery of life and death in the context of the Sacred Mysteries—the Mass—the mystery of Christ's life and death. Yet I have this nagging fear that the growing emphasis on personalization at funerals is threatening to upstage the Mass. Occasionally I hear about the death of a lifelong Catholic whose funeral does not include Mass, just some applicable Scripture readings and eulogies and warm reminiscences and loving testimonies given by friends and relatives. And I'm sad, really sad. Shouldn't a funeral be an opportunity to reflect on something greater than an individual life before tumbling back out into the quotidian soccer games, team meetings and streaming traffic?

Of course, I want it both ways when I die. Not only do I want those paying their respects to get a healthy dose of *Dies Irae,* but also I'd like a warm, fuzzy eulogy (with a positive spin, of course). I hope that part of that eulogy will include that I—admittedly all too late in life—learned to look at the temptations I faced. Sometimes I succumbed to them. Other times, I overcame them. They helped me discern who I was—with all my weaknesses, and yes, gifts. But did I use them according to God's plan? I want everyone in attendance to be reminded: Only He knows. . . .

## Questions for Reflection and Discussion

1. Have you noticed "seasons" in your prayer life? in your involvement in your parish?

2. How can considering the proper spirit for fasting and "offering it up" change the way you approach these traditions?

3. What do we owe one another in the way we support our parishes and the broader Catholic community with our money and our time?

4. How can you avoid the slippery slope to sporadic or non-attendance at Sunday Mass when your parish community is not nourishing you?

5. Over the years how have your expectations and relationships with your parish priests changed?

6. Do our traditions and rituals draw you to intimacy with God?

# Part III

## *Still Growing*

# Learning from the Good Who Didn't Die Young

"What's a nice kid like you doing in a place like this?" the old man cackled as he took my hand and shook it firmly with both of his. He asks me that every time I see him.

Although I'm hardly a kid, my weakness for this kind of flattery probably helps me to keep coming back with a group of parish volunteers who regularly visit the patients in this and other nursing homes.

But every once in a while, I too am surprised I am in a place like that. I know there are many more glamorous, worthy causes to give time to. Occasionally I'm reminded of how difficult it used to be for me to be around the sick and aged. The obvious scars on minds and bodies left by bad health and too much time was often more than I could bear. And I would still be unable to give my time to this work had I not discovered that dealing with sick and failing old people is a skill that can be *learned*.

The lessons began for me when my friend Kay trapped me into filling out a group of volunteers she was organizing to visit the nursing homes in our parish. When I attended that first social—a Christmas party—I made it clear this was for "one time only"—a repayment for a favor.

The following day Kay telephoned me, bursting with enthusiasm over the party. "Wasn't that *fun?*" she asked.

I was most positive in telling her that it was not. I told her how upset I was by the poor man in the corner who wept whenever someone looked at him. And if anyone asked him what was wrong, he started all over again. I couldn't adequately explain my feeling of helplessness. I admitted I just couldn't keep my composure with the woman who thought I was her daughter or the lady next to her who kept trying to send me to the store every time I passed by with the cookies. Then there was the old woman who greeted me tearfully in Slovak, embraced me and told me everything that must have happened to her in the last 83 years, leaving me totally speechless. I didn't even mention how eerie I found those people who sat there, silently staring into space.

Kay laughed. "I can tell you've never had any experience with old people. Haven't you ever been around any elderly relatives?"

I said I had not, and I secretly hoped I would never have to be.

Kay must have thought I had potential despite my lack of enthusiasm, and shortly after that, over coffee, she shared some knowledge she had gained as a geriatric nurse. She explained that stroke victims often express all kinds of emotions by crying because it's the only response left to them. "You don't know if they're really sad," she said. "They may be glad to see you. Crying could be their only way of expressing gratitude for your company. It can also be simply an emotional release." She went on to tell me that if I could accept the tears as just a means of communication, I would find them less disturbing.

That seemed reasonable, and so did her suggestion for dealing with the demented and forgetful patients: to respond to them as I would like people to respond to me. Suddenly it made sense to go along gently with a confused person's idea that I was a daughter or an old friend, rather than go through the frustrating and futile exercise of trying to explain over and over that I was not.

The next time the volunteer group returned to visit, I went with them.

As I gradually stopped worrying about my feelings, I discovered that my subsequent visits to the nursing homes were more relaxed and even occasionally enjoyable. I noticed, too, that the word was getting around. A lot of other parishioners were beginning to volunteer. We were *learning!*

Our parish promoted the nursing home outreach in its bulletin. Soon there were regular bingo parties, and many parishioners who couldn't visit donated handmade and purchased prizes for the games. A parish committee sent birthday cards to all the patients. The students in the parish school of religion made and sent valentines and other seasonal greetings. Volunteers escorted groups of ambulatory patients to local diners and parish drama club dress rehearsals. Several children from the parish school played musical instruments and sang at monthly liturgies celebrated in the nursing homes.

Unsolicited money for the nursing home activities began to come in, presenting a special challenge to the volunteers. We had to think of things to do with it. One of the regular nursing home volunteers suggested that a particular donation be used for corsages for Mother's Day. When the florist received the order, he was so impressed that he donated his labor and billed us only for the cost of his materials. The nursing homes' women patients, including those who were not mothers, received corsages. And they were delighted!

I became aware of the curious fact that in our highly civilized society, we teach each other to accept the mentally retarded, the physically handicapped, the poor and those of different cultures and races. But we are too busy or too afraid to educate ourselves to accept an even more universal condition—old age.

Accepting old people means taking them as they are, not as we think they should be. Kay reminded me of this once when I found some patients particularly depressing. "They don't *like* being grouchy and bossy and having their thoughts wander!" she said. "Would you?"When I learned to be objective about these things, I didn't take them personally, and I stopped letting annoyance—or even worse, pity—get in the way of the work I was doing.

The next thing I had to learn was old people need to be touched. I don't know why I was surprised to discover this, because it is logical that age doesn't exempt one from the need for physical signs of affection. Since people confined to nursing homes miss their husbands or wives, children and grandchildren, brothers and sisters, others have to help fill that need.

This became dramatically real to me during one of the monthly Masses during the Sign of Peace. Following the lead of others, I embraced each old man and woman. As I came to the last one, any doubts I had entertained about the value of this expression were eliminated by the woman who held me back as I started to move on and whispered in my ear, "May God give you everything that is good in this life!" Somehow I felt that for such a small gesture, I had been awarded a blessing that belonged to someone much more deserving.

At last, I learned to laugh. Funny things—no, *hilarious* things—happen in nursing homes. And why not? Each nursing home is a community in itself. Each is alive with spats, joys, rumors and in-jokes. Yet I couldn't see or appreciate this until my self-consciousness disappeared. I began to savor stories of other volunteers' funny experiences, and then I started to collect a few of my own.

It was natural to laugh—and I was delighted I could—when a very demented woman gazed up at the priest bending over to give her ashes on Ash Wednesday and breathed at him, "Hi, Honey!" And I couldn't suppress a chuckle when, at that awkward moment when Mass in an informal setting ends, and no one knows quite what to say, a man broke the silence with, "That was *real nice*, Reverend!"

Because I was willing to learn, I have had the privilege of witnessing astonishing heroism in some people who, despite tremendous physical limitations, manage to be more concerned with others' troubles rather than their own. I have seen a man trapped in his severely palsied body converse rapidly and intelligently by pointing to letters, words, numbers and pictograms painted on his wheelchair tray. And I have sung with a woman who couldn't speak well enough to carry on a conversation, but who was mysteriously able to sing at Mass in a clear, lovely and perfectly articulate voice.

There are still times when, on our regular visiting days, I can think of other things I would rather do, when my own troubles and routine seem more than enough to fill my day. But I go. This is one of the few times when it is immediately evident to me that it is in giving that we receive. And if the lessons I continue to learn weren't enough, it's always nice—on any kind of day—to have someone call me a "kid."

# ✻ It's A Sign! ✻

Many Gospel stories mystify and perplex me, but none intrigues me more than the one about the apostles fishing all night and catching nothing. The account is roughly the same in Luke (5:4-12) and John (21:1-12), and as the story goes, Jesus told the discouraged men to lower their nets again. This time they brought up a tremendous catch. So far, so good, but here's where I don't get it: After they hauled in the fish, Peter and his crew left their boats and followed Him. Were they *crazy*? Why didn't they immediately head back out to sea, lower their nets again and again, hire on some new hands, purchase a few more boats, employ even more fishermen, and establish The Really Big Time Galilean Fishing Company? After all, wasn't the load of fish *A Sign*, one validating their efforts?

I've been in the same boat. Many times throughout my life, I've sat glumly without a catch. My work doesn't satisfy me; it doesn't seem to have much meaning. Nothing I do seems to be working out. I gaze at the water and wonder what I should be DOING with my life. *Please God, send me A Sign.*

So I'm puzzled by the apostles' response to their sudden good fortune. I can't imagine they were all that different from the rest of us. They must have wondered what the future held for them. Perhaps some had been staring at the water, thinking that one more fish-less day would be *A Sign.* Then they would change careers, go into carpentry or maybe tent-making.

It seems to be an enduring characteristic of human nature that we look for signs to help us direct our lives. Ancient Romans and Greeks took note of birds' flight formations as part of their decision-making process. Today people commonly describe turning points, exclaiming that at a critical moment they observed a particular natural phenomenon—a timely rainbow, snowfall or sunset. ("I just knew this was *A Sign,* so I. . . .") Significant newspaper space is given to astrology, alerting readers to *signs* before they pour their second cup of coffee. Psychics' websites get phenomenal numbers of hits from surfers looking for *signs.* We look in the strangest places for signs to help us make choices, but nonetheless, we look.

We need signs. Without them we could wind up in Milwaukee when we wanted to go to Green Bay. We could fall off a subway platform and touch the third rail. But we also want signs to do more than keep us from getting lost or getting hurt. We hope they can provide other services—

personal risk management, validating our aspirations, preventing failure, or saving us from embarrassment. Remember how the highly risk-averse Pharisees came out to see Jesus after He had fed the multitude with a few loaves and fishes and asked Him to show them a sign from heaven? In response, Jesus "sighed deeply . . . Why does this generation ask for a sign?" (Mark 8:11-12). Scripture doesn't tell us so, but surely He must have been thinking, ". . . just like every generation. . . ."

So, generation after generation reads tea leaves, watches how the smoke rises, rolls the dice, picks petals off a daisy, divines the meaning of the page where the Bible drops open, or lays out the cards. After all, it's easier to trust random chance or to search the horizon for a message, for direction or validation than to search our hearts. *A Sign* will save us a great deal of work.

But shouldn't we be more active in our approach?

Jeremiah gives us a good lesson on how to look for and interpret signs in his beautiful metaphor of the potter forming clay (Jer 18:1-6), which is often used for homilies and reflection. The introduction is interesting and—I think—critical: "The Lord told Jeremiah to go to the potter's house; there a divine message *(A Sign)* awaited him."

My guess is that Jeremiah simply had a sudden urge to go to the potter's house to see what he was doing. Then, as he watched the potter working the clay, he had this tremendous insight, which he applied to Israel, and to all of God's people. That insight was *A Sign!* Jeremiah recognized it as such by pondering what he saw at the potter's. Then, reflecting on it later, he linked the insight with his strange urge to wander into the potter's workshop in the first place. Finally he understood Who prompted that urge.

Like Jeremiah's, our best inspirations come from insights. Those are the *Signs* inviting us to take leave of ourselves—for a moment, a year, a lifetime. They can guide us for the short term or send us off on a longer mission or possibly a new vocation. However, even if an insight comes suddenly, understanding the message requires our time, reflection and ultimately, our surrender.

The apostles, too, used insight to interpret their bountiful catch. After listening to Jesus urge them to put the nets into the water one more time, they drew up more than fish. They had a sudden insight. What they had heard Him say up to that point at last made sense, and they could see where they were being led. They didn't use this sign to validate what *they* had decided they already wanted.

Both Old Testament and New are full of stories of signs—signs well interpreted, signs disregarded. In some respect these stories do us a disservice, tempting us to look for the same kinds of signs revealed to the prophets and the apostles. Biblical signs seem so overt, so clear, that it is tempting to expect the same type of obvious revelation to come to us. But are we missing the point? The real lesson they teach, over and over, is how to look for and interpret signs when we feel adrift. These stories tell us to listen for God's prompts, whether they be to wander into the potter's studio or put our nets down one more time. Only then will we recognize *The Sign*—deep within us.

# ✾ Keeping up the Image ✾

The Mercedes streaked across the intersection, barely slowing for the stop sign. It was a red convertible, the really, really expensive model—you know—the one with the elegantly engineered roll-bar that pops up to save you when you lose control going around a curve at 100 m.p.h. My dog and I, attempting to cross at the corner, had to leap back to the curb for safety. Somewhat shaken, I glared gimlet-eyed at the car zipping down the quiet residential street. I . . . I simply couldn't hold it together. Out of control, I just could not suppress the thought: *You'd look good in that car!*

Funny, because I don't care much about cars. The one I drive is more or less an inheritance. I probably will drive it until the wheels fall off. When that moment arrives, I'll buy something off the lot, focusing on the bargain more than my image. But wait a minute. Even if I drive my present vehicle until it morphs into a Beater and finally replace it with a 2010 V-6 Such-a-Deal, I'm nurturing an image, too.

Image. What does it take to create one? When I was in college there was a very popular theology professor, Father Dan, who was never seen without his briefcase. He was a

Dominican friar and wore a white habit whenever he was on campus. The habit *cum* briefcase made him, well, distinctive, and he always referred to that briefcase as his "image." What can I say? except, it worked for him.

Popular culture teaches us that we can purchase an image. The car. Make-up. Clothes. The street-where-you-live. Manners. College degrees. Briefcases. But the old Baltimore Catechism (Lesson 5, Question 48—it's amazing what you can find on the Internet!) taught me something quite different: I am made in the image and likeness of God. The image is there from the get-go; I don't have to buy it. Yet even as I memorized that answer, I was troubled because if I genuinely believed it, I would have to have an image of God first, then an image of self. I spent much of third grade pondering this.

By fourth grade I skipped right on to the easier task of creating my self-image. By sixth grade I was into maintenance.

What is it about human nature that makes us so desperate to create a self-image? Maybe it comes from knowing that an image is a stimulus that provokes a response. Born clueless, we soon realize that people respond to externals: what we wear and how we wear it, what we drive and how we drive it, where we live and if our home looks like Martha Stewart comes in regularly to tidy up. Our self images give us power, and help us buy our way into a group. They speak in code. They grease the skids for recognition—both ways. Even the Israelites, when they asked Samuel to appoint a king for them, admitted they wanted one because they yearned to be like everyone else.

Self-images are comfortable. Whether "good" or "poor" they have accessories that surround our psyche like leather seats, heads-up panel displays, global positioning devices, and—most important—roll bars. They make us feel safe in our chosen environment. They help us go places if they are "good," or keep us in our place if they are "poor."

I saw the car again. This time I was in my own car, and both of us were approaching a four-way stop at right angles to one another. In addition to commanding the respect due this atypical car for my neighborhood, the red Mercedes convertible had the right of way. It wasn't going to be a contest anyway because I was dying to see who was driving. However, as I let it go by, I couldn't tell whether the driver was male or female, young or old. The top was up, and the windows were deep tinted glass.

Now I had to refine my original thought: yes, I'd look good in that car, but since anyone could be driving that car, wouldn't anyone look good in that car? Take, for example, the daughter of a neighborhood acquaintance. A poor self-image case, if I ever saw one. Breaking her parents' hearts and shattering the image they hoped for her, she dropped out of high school, has tattoos running up both her arms that look like they were imprinted with a #2 pencil, and a beautiful baby girl whose birth certificate does not bear the father's name. Then, there is the neighbor whose obsession with a rock star has her running to his concerts, hanging out in a bar he sometimes visits, and in the process neglecting her family who aches to see her as wife and mother. And how about the clerk in the post office who slams patrons' packages on the scale, never makes eye contact and acts if we are disturbing his otherwise pleasant day? Would their self-images be changed if they were behind the wheel of this expensive car? Would I see them differently?

Images tend to take on a life of their own. As I said, by sixth grade I was into maintenance. By then I had picked out the crowd I wanted to run with and dressed and acted like them as my allowance and baby-sitting earnings allowed. Truthfully, I haven't changed much since. The crowd is pretty much the same, even though I have pitched my tent in different cities over the years. A lot of my spending has been carefully allocated so when I show up in a new town I can establish my position, "speak" the code, and find the crowd. If I'm honest about it, this has been my life's work.

Yet that old catechism question/answer continues to haunt me: *We are made in the image and likeness of God.* Maybe I shouldn't have been so dismissive in fourth grade. Just because as a child I could not envision God as God must truly be, I let myself off the hook prematurely. Could it be that my searching, creating and maintaining my self-image since age 10 has been my way of ducking the responsibility of figuring out what God sees in ME?

This takes me back to Samuel. When the chosen one, Saul, just didn't work out, and Samuel, having no options left, had to anoint someone as king, God instructed him to pass up Jesse's first seven sons—all looking very good. Then, when Jesse admitted there was indeed a Number Eight, David, and called him in from the pasture, God told Samuel to anoint this one. Clearly the selection was not driven by the image David presented to those assembled, because he probably needed—at the very least—a bath.

But "God sees what is in the heart." In other words, He saw something the others didn't. And He liked what He saw: *His* image.

If I truly believe I am created in the image and likeness of God, I need to think about this story (1 Samuel 16:6-13). I need to pick up where I left off in third grade. If I don't, I'll forever be behind the wheel of a life-vehicle with the top up and deep tinted windows that never really reveal the driver.

While the old catechism taught me I didn't have to purchase that "image and likeness of God" because it came, after all, as part of the package, that manual didn't drive home the need and considerable cost for maintenance. If I've learned anything from my experience with my self-created image, it's that I must invest in and allocate my interior resources for the necessary maintenance of God's image. I need to keep the tank full of compassion, forgiveness and hope. I have to lubricate with grace that delicate mechanism that deploys the roll-bar, because images are fragile, prone to accidents at high speeds and sharp curves.

Which reminds me: Father Dan, as I heard at a class reunion, turned in his habit. I wonder what happened to the briefcase.

# If the Wedding Garment Fits . . .

I have to leave for the wedding at 5:30 p.m. It is now noon. So I have five and a half-hours in which to sew the outfit I'm going to wear. (I'm not exaggerating, by the way. If anything, I'm being a little generous in defining the time window.) The event is a Laotian feast celebrating the marriage of Kai, my daughter-in-law's brother. Loosely speaking, I'm "family," and I'm invited. The fact that everyone is "family" in this culture is beside the point.

With her charming way that melts all possible resistance, Syphachanh suggested I might like to wear a *sinh* to the party. This is a very simple, elegant silk brocade wrap-skirt. I have thought *sinh* gorgeous since the first time I saw *The King and I*. As soon as I replied that-would-be-nice, Sypha whisked out a stunning piece of green and gold material. It took me a moment to realize it was raw fabric that had yet to be fashioned into the skirt. Sypha saw my hesitation. "I'll have someone sew it for you," she offered. I envisioned her mother, sisters and a flock of friends—I mean, family—busily preparing for the feast, still a couple of days away. "No, no!" I insisted. "If you leave me a finished *sinh* to copy, I can sew it myself."

Well, the two-day window shrank to five and a half-hours for a variety of reasons, mostly involving what top I could wear with it and maybe we should get another fabric-how-do-you-like-blue? Just before noon on the day of the wedding, Sypha produced a blouse for me that sealed the decision: the green fabric was A Go.

My son, daughter-in-law and grandsons have left my house for an early round of the festivities, so now I am alone with the fabric, Sypha's own wedding *sinh* for a sample, my very dusty sewing machine, and a lot of second thoughts.

While I admired *sinh*, did I really want to wear one? They look fabulous on the Southeast Asian women, but on *me?* My hips are too broad; my hair is too curly; my skin is much too pale. Will I look silly, as though I'm trying to be something I'm not? Will I seem presumptuous, rudely intruding on another's culture?

I think of Sypha's perpetual generosity to me, so I start to work. Really, this should be fairly simple—piece of cake, actually. I set aside my concerns about how I'm going to look and focus on doing a good job. I decide to put a lining in it, like the sample. I know I don't have to, and the effort will cost me some time, but lining the skirt will make it hang more evenly and wear better. Hmmm. French seams! O.K. That will take me more time, but I can craft them if I carefully think the procedure through. I inspect the sample with closer scrutiny. Good grief! I hadn't noticed those darts! By this point I have sewn the material into a large tube, and I hop inside and hold it up, trying to figure out where those little stitched-down tucks should go. (To get the picture, imagine having fabric suspended from a flexible hula-hoop around your waist. You know there have to be some darts sewn in *somewhere* to get the garment to fit smoothly over your hips without bunching, and you must still have a sizeable section left over to lap in a fold across the front of your body.) I think of that nice rose-pink jacket dress hanging in my closet. The one I was planning to wear in the first place. . . .

Then, while I clearly have more urgent things to focus on, I suddenly GET it—something that has simmered on my mind's back burner for years: the mystery of the silent man. He's the one who shows up near the end of the parable in St. Matthew's gospel about the wedding feast. When the invited guests wouldn't come and the angry king sent his servants to round up some street people and issue them

wedding garments so they'd look presentable, one man got
to the table without the proper garb (Mt 22:11-12). "The
king asked, 'How did you get in here, my friend, without a
wedding garment?' And the man was silent."

Silent. I think about this as I sew. Why didn't the man
say anything, especially since in the early part of the
story, the invited guests babbled one excuse after another? But he was silent. Silent. Really, what could be sim-
pler than to put on a white robe or even a *sinh?* Then it
occurred to me that this man, this "guest," while poor,
was no fool. When you look closely at the wedding garment, you see it is full of subtleties. The placement of the
darts and seams reveals your shape. There is a pattern in
the weave that needs attention when you put the garment on so it looks like you are wearing it thoughtfully.
And this guest must have had other . . . could we say,
issues? Was he too proud to wear something loaned or
donated? Was he reluctant to cross a cultural chasm?
Did he usurp the king's role and make the decision that
he wouldn't really fit in, even if he were dressed to look
like the others? Or did he feel compelled to make a
statement of his own individuality by standing apart
from the crowd? The requirement of the wedding gar-

ment really wasn't a simple request after all. It was complex, and he refused. He had his reasons. . . .

And he had his pride.

I know—in a small way—that if only he had left his pride at the door and worn the garment, how warmly he would have been welcomed. When I got to Kai's wedding (grateful to the inventor of the safety pin), Sypha and her family were obviously pleased that I had worn the *sinh*. I saw that by accepting the gift, I was saying that I had accepted them. And all the while I had worried about being accepted *by* them!

In his bountiful and perpetual generosity, God (the king in the parable), invites us to His Feast. He accepts us and welcomes us as friends and offers us something "foreign" to wear so all can identify us as His guests. He encourages us to savor the "garment's" subtleties, taking an entire lifetime if we wish. He promises us that this Feast of mutual giving and acceptance is eternal, one we share intimately, as family. All we have to do is put aside our pride and slip the wedding garment on.

# ❉ *Why Me, Lord? . . .* ❉

Count your blessings! How many times have you heard someone say that to you? How many times have you said it to others? It is one of those things we repeat to remind ourselves that, even in times of trouble, we should be grateful for the good things we have—health, employment, our children, a nice home, a trouble-free automobile, an education. . . .

But stop counting for just a moment. What do we mean when we talk about our blessings?

The word *blessing*—the thing, rather than the action—means a token or gift given to demonstrate divine favor. If we thoughtfully examine this definition, we can see that sometimes we use the word carelessly without thinking about the far-reaching implications of its meaning.

A priest recently told his congregation at Sunday Mass about a special liturgy he had celebrated for a large group of invalids and handicapped people. "People were brought in on stretchers and in wheelchairs. The blind were led in by service dogs. Many came on crutches. It was very moving," he said, "and it made me think of how often we forget to count our blessings."

The priest did not intend to imply that the lame and the blind were less favored by God than the healthy, well-fed, well-educated, sighted crowd listening to his words at that moment. However, because the way we often use the word *blessing,* it could seem that way.

Old Testament writers frequently showed that God rewarded loyal people with material things. It was a simple and dramatic way of making the point that God blesses his friends. However, we should be careful about using the word *blessing* to refer to the things that life gives to us that are apparently good. There is a danger that we may be tempted to believe that the most beautiful, talented, richest, smartest people on Earth must be the most favored by God. We could also risk feeling so "blessed" ourselves that we can't deal with trouble when it comes along.

One of our parish pastoral care ministers tells a story that demonstrates this dramatically. "Agnes was very depressed by her stroke. I knew from her family that she was deeply religious. She attended Mass whenever she was able, but never received Communion, either at Mass or when I would bring it with me on my visits. She didn't want to go to confession or receive the Sacrament of the Sick, either.

"After many visits with her, prayers with her and for her, I suddenly thought of what might be at the root of her depression. I knew she had led a very comfortable life materially, and she had once been an accomplished pianist. Now all of this had been taken away. One day, I asked if she thought her illness was a punishment from God. She burst into tears and told me that she didn't know what she could have done to deserve such a curse. She had always enjoyed so many blessings. And now she felt that surely she must be a terrible person. We talked about how things just happen to us in life, because we are human, and that we are called to deal with them—the good things and the bad. Then she agreed to see our pastor and have him hear her confession. Since then she has had fewer days of depression. I have no doubt that now she doesn't think of her illness as a curse. Maybe, in time, she will even look on it as an opportunity for spiritual blessings."

We don't know why God permits evil in the world. The writer Flannery O'Connor once said, "Evil is not a problem to be solved, but a mystery to be endured." The same is true for the good in life. We don't know why God permits some people to have a lot of material "blessings." One interesting and not often mentioned aspect of the story of

Job is that he made the mistake of presuming he knew what was on God's mind when God took away his material things. God lets Job carry on about this to his friends for a good number of pages before finally setting him straight.

Job's sufferings turned out to be a blessing in disguise. Agnes' may too. We all have had occasion to describe an experience in this way. The person who lost a job and was forced to change career direction, and then came out better and happier than if he had stayed employed, has said it. People who discover a special peace when suffering severe illness have said it.

It seems to be a paradox that we call these kinds of tragedies "blessings," when at the same time we call the good things in life "blessings." But we can do this if we look at the events and things in our lives as simply—events and things. These happen to everyone. This is the way life is. However, if we accept these things of life—good and bad—as opportunities for some special kind of growth, then they can bring blessings. Taking this point of view about the good things in our lives helps us keep from becoming smug, from taking our "blessings" for granted and from believing that God has given us these things because we are smarter, better, holier or somehow more deserving than others.

I have a friend who lives a comfortable suburban life and who believes that because she and her neighbors enjoy nice things, they are cursed. She feels that we must be poor and suffering to get to heaven. "I think someday that we will pay for this," she told me. The people she refers to are good, church-going folks, and they would be shocked by her conclusion.

So would Jesus. He didn't condemn the rich for possessing things, but He did tell them—and us—that we must share what we have. He taught a lack of emotional dependence on material things, an attitude of detachment that requires an enormous trust in God. He also holds us accountable for the things that have been given to us. At the end of the parable of the servants waiting with their lamps lit for their master's return, Jesus says, "When a man has had a great deal given to him, a great deal will be demanded of him; when a man has had a great deal given him in trust, even more will be expected of him" (Luke 12:35-48).

This challenges us to share our blessings in some way that shows God we realize that the good fortune we enjoy is a gift with strings attached. This could mean taking in a foster child. It could mean doing volunteer work rather than looking for a paying job when the family doesn't really need more money. It could mean teaching religion, visiting the sick, listening to someone in trouble. Thomas Merton made a point worth remembering when he said, "In order to know and love God through his gifts, we have to use them as if we used them not, and yet we have to *use* them." (Italics his)

But my friend's words serve as a warning that the good things we often call blessings sometimes could be bad for us. This can happen if we selfishly use them simply for our own indulgence, comfort and pleasure, and consider them essential to our own importance.

Wealth, especially, can be a real problem. The Gospels have many stories of the difficulties the rich will have in attaining heaven. Sometimes though, it is hard to translate the wealth of gospel characters who possessed servants, jewels, vineyards and livestock into our riches of household appliances, supermarkets and cars.

One night our family was watching a TV feature on life in Palm Springs, California. I was surprised when my fifteen-year-old son said, "I wouldn't want to be that rich." When I asked him why, he replied, "Because I couldn't handle it."

I was impressed with his wisdom and self-knowledge—particularly because I just had been dreaming how nice it *would* be to be that rich! But he brought me back to the reality that dealing with wealth is a special kind of burden. This is evident in the well-publicized, troubled lives of entertainment figures and athletes who suddenly "make it." They are often quick to point out that wealth hasn't been the blessing they thought it would be.

"God doesn't give us anything more than we can handle." How often we say that one, too! But have you ever thought of using that expression to describe your blessings as well as your troubles? Most of us reading this book enjoy good health, job opportunities, educational opportunities, worship opportunities, nice homes, cars, abundant food. Are these more than we can handle? Do we deal with these "blessings" as purposefully as we deal with our troubles?

The key to understanding what material blessings really mean in our lives lies in a question we usually ask when trouble brings us down: "Why me, Lord?" If we ask this about every blessing we have, we will see that each one has a special meaning for us, and that we are called to do more than just be grateful. Our material blessings give us opportunities for spiritual blessings—more than we can count.

## Sometimes Your Best Friends
## DO Tell You

My two friends have been searching for a long time. They need a place to worship. He was brought up in a rigid Baptist tradition; she was brought up in a rigid Catholic tradition. I am not reporting on their search, because, well, it is theirs. While I can identify with their search in many ways, my own search has never taken me outside of Catholicism. So I can't speak about their unique experience and what they are hoping to find.

But today they told me they went to Mass at my parish. I was quite surprised, but, of course, delighted. When you are happy with your home, you want to gather people in. And when you are secure in your belief that yours is Truly Home, well, you want to make sure people not only feel welcome, but you want to make them comfortable enough to stay and share your Food.

"What did you think?" I asked.

She commented on how much the liturgy has changed since she last attended Mass more than 30 years ago. Not realizing the difference between the Nicene Creed and the Apostles Creed, she felt confused. He wondered if there were any prayer books, and if so, where were they kept; he had wanted to follow along.

Then we got to the serious stuff. "I felt like I was in a bus station," he confessed. "And, before the service was over, people apparently knew the buses were getting ready to leave, because half the people in the church filed out." She said the congregation struck her as being very preoccupied.

"What's 7:30 a.m. Mass like?" she asked. Before I could respond, he interjected, "Is it more reverent?"

I mumbled something about liturgical styles, suggesting 7:30 was unquestionably more "quiet." But I felt sick. Suddenly I saw my parish as my friends saw it: noisy, distracted and distracting, irreverent, badly dressed, and appearing nonchalant about what was happening at the altar.

My friends are not complainers. They softened their remarks by telling me they had visited a neighboring Catholic parish and observed the same bustling, casual atmosphere. I knew they spoke the truth. I've been troubled by such concerns for years. Yet I've pushed these thoughts to the background. "Be glad people volunteer," I say to myself when I see Eucharistic ministers dressed as though they just rushed in from working in their gardens. "Be grateful that they bring the kids at all," I think when children unload snacks, Legos, crayons and coloring books, dolls and toy trucks from their backpacks. "Teenagers are going through a stage," I insist silently when the girl in the pew ahead of me combs her hair all through Mass and others talk and giggle audibly during the Eucharistic prayer. "Focus on her lovely voice," I remind myself when the young woman leading the congregational singing raises her arm and with it the short sweater she has on, which invites everyone in the church to stare at her navel.

"But what about the hospitality of this parish?" its defenders would protest, and I become one such defender. Every warm body is welcome here, not only to worship with us, but also to sign up for anything at any time. At least a third of the registered adults are involved in some kind of parish activity. And the financial support is extremely generous. As a parish, we dig deep, and dig often. We contribute unstintingly in good times and in bad. Our largesse is immune to the ups and downs of our nation's economy and our nation's bishops. . . .

But do we pride ourselves on our hospitality, social service activities and financial generosity at the expense of reverence? And, in a companion question: has reverence been a casualty of the revision of the liturgy that followed Vatican II? Could it be that increased lay participation, which makes liturgies lively and full of activity, has led us to forget that these are still the *Sacred* Mysteries, *Holy* Mass celebrated in the *sanc*tuary. Isn't it still, Holy-Holy-Holy?

As I ponder these things, without coming up with satisfactory answers, suddenly I'm struck with another question—one more challenging yet: Why should my friends expect to find reverence at Mass? They are seasoned church shoppers. I know they've tested every denomination known to urban humanity. They know there are lots of different styles of worship. They've been to churches that literally rock with contemporary music. They've been to churches where the community simply sits in meditation. They've heard rousing preachers. They've . . . well, done it all. But they expected reverence in this Catholic parish. Do they know something that we, as a Catholic community, don't comprehend, something we may have forgotten, or something we have taken so much for granted that we have become inured to its reality and its power?

Even if we come to Mass harried, frazzled and time-starved, isn't it the Holy-Holy-Holy that we genuinely seek, deep down, as do my friends? We come to get our Food for the week—the Ultimate Take-Out, the spiritual nourishment that sanctifies the work we do and the sustenance we need to bring the Good News to others. Yet how can we invite others to share in the sacred mystery of This Bread, This Cup, if we don't demonstrate by our reverence that we believe this mystery is true and awesome?

The solution is really simple, a variant on a comment Fr. Cletus, our associate pastor, made one morning at early Mass. As he was about to begin the Eucharistic prayer, he told us that as a seminarian, he was told he should, for the rest of his life, celebrate every Mass as if it were his first. How would it be then, for us, if we attended every Mass as if it were our last?

# Sometimes I Haven't Got a Prayer

Books about prayer inspire me—to incredible feelings of inadequacy. They remind me of some old high school anxieties. In those days teen magazines, with their glitzy articles and glamorous models, convinced me I'd never have the right clothes, the right make-up, the right hairstyle, or be the right weight to belong to the right crowd.

So it is today with books on prayer. Whether their focus is on active liturgical practices or contemplative prayer, I admire them from a safe distance, knowing if I made an attempt to apply what I read, I'd wind up feeling as if I'm genuflecting on the wrong knee.

Yet I, like many today, hunger for new expressions of spirituality. We American Catholics have an unprecedented willingness to learn from other cultures many different ways to approach God. I suppose that is good. No, I *know* that is good. But my struggle is this: I can intellectually appreciate an unfamiliar type of prayer, but I resist trying it, and thus stir up a vague sense of guilt.

It's always convenient to blame a problem of this kind on one's upbringing, and so I will. While I hesitate to call Mother Church's pre-Vatican II style dysfunctional, it did set up certain barriers to exploring a variety of prayer modes. In spite of the *Baltimore Catechism's* mention of mental prayer under "Kinds of Prayer," it supported (or perhaps it established) the prevailing attitude of our teachers and Church officials of that day: Interior, deeply intimate, connection with God was reserved for saints, and not-to-worry, they were all dead. All we ordinary folk had to do was stay within the Guard Rails. Thus we would live good, but not necessarily holy lives, and in doing so squeak though the pearly gates.

So how did prayer fit in that program? Well, there was the Mass (obviously), the Rosary (probably), novenas (big time), litanies (lots), Stations of the Cross (seasonal), the Divine Office (clergy only, please), and the Little Office of the Blessed Virgin Mary (for vowed religious and the professionally pious). That about did it. Oh, I nearly forgot: the Act of Contrition (don't leave consciousness without it).

When I reflect on my training and review that old catechism to make sure I wasn't simply imagining things, I can see how formulaic it made prayer. The catechism neatly laid out the subject in a question and answer format. Even the definition was organized as though it could have been a Power Point presentation:

Q. What is prayer?

A. Prayer is the lifting up of our minds and hearts to God,

- to adore Him
- to thank Him for His benefits
- to ask His forgiveness
- and to beg of Him all the graces we need whether for soul or body.

(*Baltimore Catechism,* Lesson Twenty-Eight: On Prayer)

The bullets are mine, but you can see there is little room for wandering about. One could (and I did) conclude the subtext was, "Now you know all there is to know about it; go do it."

What a different approach to prayer our current catechism suggests! A tip-off in the change in attitude comes in its definition of prayer, a quotation from St. Thérèse of Lisieux:

> "For me, prayer is a surge of the heart; it is a simple
> look turned toward heaven;
> it is a cry of recognition and of love, embracing both
> trial and joy."

This sets a new tone—a spirituality of wings rather than one of knees firmly planted on the ground. I get the message, but now, where do I go?

I pick up books on centering prayer, Pentecostal prayer, *lectio divina,* the Enneagram, new meditations for the Rosary, creative liturgies and prayer services, and how to compose inspiring invocations for any occasion. But again that old insecurity begins to well up. I balk because it seems to me that every writer about prayer—contemporary or ancient—seems, so . . . *sure.* It strikes me they are, in their own ways, as formulaic as the *Baltimore Catechism.* Simon Tugwell, O.P., notes in the introduction to his book, *Ways of Imperfection,* that he omitted discussion of several spiritual writers of the sixteenth century because their influence on subsequent spirituality was "almost tyrannical." I know just what he means.

He makes me feel better. But I have to admit that doesn't let me off the hook. The fact that I'm bothered by interior nagging about the state of my prayer life calls me to look deeper. I have to admit I've been content to stay within the Guard Rails. I've been more than content. Upon reaching adulthood, I began to add boards to the Guard Rails, so in effect, I turned them into ramparts. My construction project has obscured all but a very narrow path—one very easily trod. And it has made me so . . . *sure.*

The spirit of the new catechism not only beckons, it instructs me to lighten up. So, I pick up some more books. Some I like. Others I don't. I relax. This is a bold, new adventure for me. Soon I begin to perceive the spirit—not just the words. And then I begin to see the Spirit.

I discover prayer should be an expression of the unique relationship that every individual has with God. "Unique" is the key word; I shouldn't expect my prayer life to be like anyone else's. But unique expression has dangers, too. If I focus exclusively on my singular relationship with God, I risk forgetting that others have their unique relationship with Him as well. Then I become, once again, so . . . *sure*.

And I see that's where traditional, formulaic prayers come in. They serve as a great unifier—with the Mass being the most perfect in that respect. These prayers call us to holy relationship with one another. And they keep us praying even when our personal prayer lacks wings.

Guard Rails. They do have their function—and not a bad one after all.

## *Questions for Reflection and Discussion*

1.  How will you know when you are "grown up" spiritually? How will you know when you have grown as far as you can?

2.  What fears and ignorance influence your response to the aged?

3.  Do you recognize some ways to bring His image and His signs into better focus after these readings?

4.  What do you need to put on or take off at this time to truly embrace the feast of life?

5.  How would it be if you attended every Mass as if it were your last?

6.  How can expanding your view of blessings and prayer contribute to the adventure of being and staying Catholic?

# Additional Titles Published by Resurrection Press, a Catholic Book Publishing Imprint

| | |
|---|---:|
| A Rachel Rosary *Larry Kupferman* | $4.50 |
| Blessings All Around *Dolores Leckey* | $8.95 |
| Catholic Is Wonderful *Mitch Finley* | $4.95 |
| Come, Celebrate Jesus! *Francis X. Gaeta* | $4.95 |
| Days of Intense Emotion *Keeler/Moses* | $12.95 |
| From Holy Hour to Happy Hour *Francis X. Gaeta* | $7.95 |
| Grace Notes *Lorraine Murray* | $9.95 |
| Healing through the Mass *Robert DeGrandis, SSJ* | $9.95 |
| Our Grounds for Hope *Fulton J. Sheen* | $7.95 |
| The Healing Rosary *Mike D.* | $5.95 |
| Healing Your Grief *Ruthann Williams, OP* | $7.95 |
| Heart Peace *Adolfo Quezada* | $9.95 |
| Life, Love and Laughter *Jim Vlaun* | $7.95 |
| The Joy of Being an Altar Server *Joseph Champlin* | $5.95 |
| The Joy of Being a Catechist *Gloria Durka* | $4.95 |
| The Joy of Being a Eucharistic Minister *Mitch Finley* | $5.95 |
| The Joy of Being a Lector *Mitch Finley* | $5.95 |
| The Joy of Being an Usher *Gretchen Hailer, RSHM* | $5.95 |
| The Joy of Marriage Preparation *McDonough/Marinelli* | $5.95 |
| The Joy of Music Ministry *J.M. Talbot* | $6.95 |
| The Joy of Preaching *Rod Damico* | $6.95 |
| The Joy of Teaching *Joanmarie Smith* | $5.95 |
| The Joy of Worshiping Together *Rod Damico* | $5.95 |
| Lights in the Darkness *Ave Clark, O.P.* | $8.95 |
| Loving Yourself for God's Sake *Adolfo Quezada* | $5.95 |
| Meditations for Survivors of Suicide *Joni Woelfel* | $5.95 |
| Mother Teresa *Eugene Palumbo, S.D.B.* | $5.95 |
| Personally Speaking *Jim Lisante* | $8.95 |
| Practicing the Prayer of Presence *Muto/van Kaam* | $8.95 |
| Prayers from a Seasoned Heart *Joanne Decker* | $8.95 |
| Praying the Lord's Prayer with Mary *Muto/vanKaam* | $8.95 |
| 5-Minute Miracles *Linda Schubert* | $4.95 |
| Season of New Beginnings *Mitch Finley* | $4.95 |
| Season of Promises *Mitch Finley* | $4.95 |
| Soup Pot *Ethel Pochocki* | $8.95 |
| St. Katharine Drexel *Daniel McSheffery* | $12.95 |
| Stay with Us *John Mullin, SJ* | $3.95 |
| Surprising Mary *Mitch Finley* | $7.95 |
| What He Did for Love *Francis X. Gaeta* | $5.95 |
| Woman Soul *Pat Duffy, OP* | $7.95 |
| You Are My Beloved *Mitch Finley* | $10.95 |
| Your Sacred Story *Robert Lauder* | $6.95 |

For a free catalog call 1-800-892-6657
www.catholicbookpublishing.com